Murphys
ICE CREAM

BOOK OF
SWEET
THINGS

MERCIER PRESS

Cork

www.mercierpress.ie

Trade enquiries to CMD Distribution,
55A Spruce Avenue, Stillorgan Industrial Park,
Blackrock, County Dublin.

ISBN: 978 1 85635 584 1

10 9 8 7 6 5 4 3 2 1

A CIP record for this title is available from the British Library

 Mercier Press receives financial assistance from the Arts
Council/An Chomhairle Ealaíon

Printed & bound in the EU.

BOOK OF
SWEET
THINGS

SEÁN AND KIERAN MURPHY

MERCIER PRESS

WHAT YOU NEED TO READ

Table of Contents:

Irish Ice Cream Recipes

Ice Cream Recipes with International Flair

Sorbet Recipes

Acknowledgments:

There are so many people who made this book possible including the entire Murphys Ice Cream team, our extended family (especially Finbarr and Sophia Christine for their amazing support and for their editing skills), Mercier Press for their help and confidence in the project, Geraldine Nichol of the Book Bureau, and our friends and neighbours in Dingle and Killarney.

Our customers deserve a special mention, not only for their custom over the years but because hundreds of them, from our local regulars, to families from Cork, Dublin and beyond, to solo food-lovers in search of perfection, have offered insight and suggestions that helped us refine these recipes.

The idea for this book came from our blog – Ice Cream Ireland (http://icecreamireland.com). Many readers and bloggers have tested recipes and made improvements including the people behind these excellent blogs: Chocolate Gourmand, Crazy Delicious, Cryptic Words Meander, dsz123.net, Eat Drink Live, The Endless Pursuit of Life, Fairy Cake Heaven, Food Rockz, I've Got Seoul, Little Bird Eats, Roscommon to Imogene, Stuff Yer Bake, Sticky Gooey Creamy Chewy, Supertaster, The Humble Housewife, and Vivre en Nouvelle-Zélande. Our readers from Ireland and around the world have also helped including Marie from Idaho, Andrea from Australia, and Karin from Holland. You know who you are, and thanks!

Curtain Call, Dingle, gave us many lovely fabrics we used for photography.

Ursula Tramski gave us the loan of the beautiful, wood-fired pottery you will see in some of the photos – www.smashingpots.com.

The internet has been a vast source of information. Thanks to all the useful sites out there including Wikipedia (for all its quirkiness).

MURPHY

PUSH

MIND YOUR STEP

Irelands Gourmet IceCream

Made in Dingle

Christmas Charity Shop

LET'S GO

Prologue:

In 1999, my brother Seán, my mother and I lingered on the bridge near Notre Dame in Paris, eating ice cream. Boats meandered down the Seine – the passengers gazing up at the mansions on the Ile St Louis. The bells chimed above us, the sun broke through the clouds, and we were happy. There is something about Paris that heightens the senses, especially when it comes to taste, and we have always loved sweet things in our family. We savoured each mouthful in silence and couldn't help smiling as the frozen raspberry, chocolate, coffee, lemon and caramel melted on our collective palates.

We met in Paris with a single purpose – to decide whether we should start an artisan ice cream company in Dingle. We had chosen France because we had talked about making ice cream that would impress not only in Ireland but that could compete with the best in the world. Seán had flown in from San Francisco and had to decide whether he wanted to give up his stable job and convertible. I had already given up on the corporate world a few years before and had settled in West Kerry. My father, a Corkman, couldn't be there because of business commitments, but my mother joined us from New York as a potential investor and source of inspiration, since she had nurtured our love of good food since we could remember.

The beginning of a new venture is always precious – full of hope and excitement. Murphys Ice Cream! The decision wasn't that hard. Life is short, and it's far, far preferable spending your work days doing something you love. When that something is sweet as well, so much the better …

Kieran Murphy

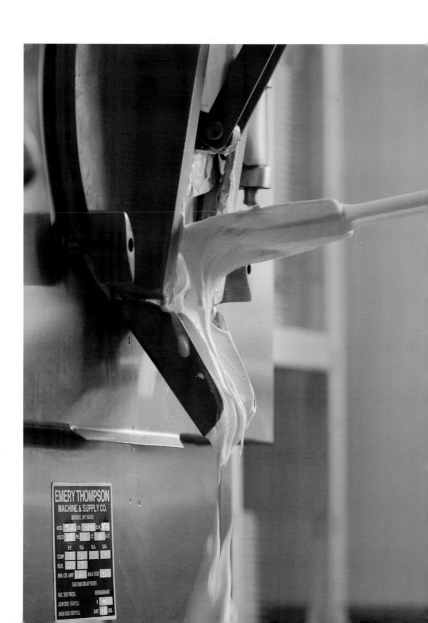

A Special Treat . . .

This is a book for all lovers of sweet things. It is meant to bring joy to you, your friends, and your family. Desserts in general, and ice cream in particular, can cheer us up when we are sad, help us celebrate a special occasion, or epitomise the pleasure of an exceptional holiday. Ice cream, especially when it is natural, fresh and made with love, is packed with all the joy, dreams and anticipation of childhood. The cold astonishes and refreshes the taste buds, the creaminess brings sensual pleasure, and the sweetness rejuvenates the soul. When Seán and I think about our Dingle and Killarney shops, when we look at the families laughing, the young and old couples holding hands over a sundae, the mother enjoying her moments of peace alone with a sorbet, we find happiness. We want to translate some of this magic and bring it into your home.

You will not find super-trendy recipes or ground-breaking science in this book. You will not find desserts designed to impress the eye at the expense of impressing the palate. Our philosophy has always been to use the best ingredients, and with great ingredients and care, you will have outstanding results. The starting point for us is Kerry milk and cream, which we consider to be the best in the world. You might prefer your own local dairy, but make sure the milk and cream are fresh. Ice cream amplifies imperfections of flavour. The same goes for the quality of your other ingredients, especially chocolate, vanilla and fruit. If you can find fresh, ripe, succulent strawberries, you can make a good strawberry ice cream. If you can't, make something else!

The final and most important ingredient is love. In this busy life of ours, when time is a precious commodity, many of us don't spend as much time as we would like in the kitchen. Yet, the simple act of cooking can awaken and nourish the creative spirit and provide a means to express love for ourselves and for those about whom we care. A great cook, professional or otherwise, imbues their dishes with love, and food made in a hurry and without due care is bound to disappoint. So, if at all possible, chisel out enough time to enjoy making (as well as eating) these desserts. Clear your mind of stress and worry, and indulge yourself. After all, no one needs to make or eat an ice cream – it's a special treat for the soul.

So, treat yourself! We hope this book will be well-worn, well-loved, spattered with chocolate and smudged with caramel sauce. It's easy to get started. Most of the recipes require no more equipment than a bowl, a hob, a pan and a spoon, although we do recommend buying a domestic ice cream machine. Many of the recipes are quite simple, and there are techniques for all of them that we will pass on. Once you get the hang of it, you will most likely never taste ice cream as good as that prepared in your own kitchen, because you can make it to suit yourself.

At Murphys Ice Cream, we think research and development is best done with a spoon and would like you to use your taste buds as your guide. Do you want to know the 'right' way to make any given dessert? It is quite simply the way that yields the best flavour. We love the recipes in this book, but ingredients vary and regional differences can change the final result. Different people also have different preferences. So trust your palate! If you think a recipe is too sweet, cut down on the sugar. If your taste buds tell you to add more alcohol, do so. If you think it would be cool to try it with a bit of black pepper, why not? Feel free to experiment, and have fun. Then, please tell us how it goes! We've designed this book as a helpful tool in the exploration of tasty treats. We hope your exploration is a joyous one.

Seán and Kieran Murphy

(You can email us through our website: www.murphysicecream.ie)

The Murphys Ice Cream Story

In April of **2000**, Seán and I stood on Strand Street in Dingle, admiring our new shop as the sign-writer balanced on his stepladder, screwing the last letter to the fascia above the front door. We had painted the outside and the insides ourselves, the plumber and electrician had finished their work, and the scooping cabinet and espresso machine came in on time from Italy. Cups, cutlery and furniture had arrived from Dublin. Newspaper still covered the windows, but we were ready for our grand opening. As the sign-writer clambered down his ladder, we saw it for the first time – 'Murphys.' We could hardly contain our excitement. A couple of old fellows wandered down the sidewalk toward us, and they stopped and looked at the shop in amazement.

'Aren't those Yanks cute, putting an Irish name above the door,' one said to the other. Then they moved on, but they weren't the only ones difficult to impress.

'So, who are you?' potential suppliers would ask us, as we pressured them for the best quality vanilla or for paper takeaway cups instead of polystyrene. 'What are you trying to do?'

Most suppliers couldn't come to terms with the idea that ice cream could be in any way gourmet or that those two crazy Yanks in Dingle had any right to be so demanding. Ice cream, when we started, was widely considered a children's indulgence. A passion for it? A dream to be the best in the world? Few of them thought it was worth the trouble. If we could get them to visit at all (Dingle is, after all, very remote), they listened to us and invariably began talking about price instead of quality. They offered us synthetic flavourings or processed egg yolks that were a quarter of the price of real eggs.

'You're foolish,' they would say, as we showed them the door. 'Do you really think an Irish person will be able to tell the difference?'

That's exactly it. We have always believed Irish people do know the difference, and our experience in business has confirmed it. Of course, we were not the only ones who had faith in the Irish palate. A number of chefs and artisan producers in Ireland consistently delivered world-class foods to appreciative customers long before we ever opened our doors, and there were suppliers who supplied them. Slowly, we found them, and they didn't ask who we were and what we were trying to do. They just got it. We still do business with almost all of them, and we wouldn't be who we are without their care and passion.

A Little Digression – Why Ice Cream?

I can't say that we grew up with the dream of starting an ice cream company, but in retrospect, it seems the most natural thing in the world. Ice cream defined our childhood. Our freezer always contained various flavours thanks to a mother with a sweet tooth, even when we became teenagers and easily ate a carton in a quick sitting.

My memory of my early years tends to be of the hazy sort, but I can remember my encounters with chocolate chip mint ice cream perfectly. It was a family favourite when I was young – light and creamy, with big, dark chocolate chunks. What I liked best was how quickly it melted, and as it did so, it became even more delicious. I remember standing in our New York kitchen, age six, stirring it in my bowl with a spoon until it turned into a soft, half-melted mass of minty perfection, and then devouring it and relishing the satisfying crunch of the chocolate chips.

Our parents enjoyed good food, especially of the fresh and natural variety, and they loved their desserts – the more indulgent the better. Although my baby formula was specially imported from Switzerland, biodynamic, and super-healthy, my first solid meal was a shared banana split from a roadside, old-school ice cream parlour in upstate New York, where we headed away for weekends. This apparent contradiction was part of our growing up – a meal of home-made vegetable burgers topped with bean sprouts, served between two thick slices of my mother's freshly-baked, organic bread, would be followed by a sumptuous Poire Belle Hélène, dripping in cream and chocolate sauce (recipe under 'Desserts).

My mother, although not often in the kitchen, revelled in exploration, and she pushed us in terms of cuisine and in accepting new tastes. As children, we might have expressed some unease when she discovered borscht or brought home vegetables neither ourselves or our friends had ever heard of, but we were just as likely to be amazed by a foray into French almond cookies or by her collecting the sap of the maple tree in the back yard to make her own maple syrup. Ingredients always mattered, and she built up a network of unusual suppliers. She would drive ten miles to collect fresh, unpasteurised milk from a maverick farmer and transform it into a decadent flan along with eggs from a clutch of organic chickens owned by a retirement home up the road.

The usual mistress of the kitchen, however, was my Aunt Carol, who had followed my father to the United States to help rear us. Her cooking was strictly Cork and quite pleasing to youngsters – her shepherd's pie and apple crumble with vanilla ice cream would balance the previous meal from my mother – free-range Cornish game hens with a soufflé of kale from the neighbour's garden. Carol's real forte was her baking, and she expected us to help. We never minded, although perhaps we spent more time licking the spoon than mixing the brownie batter. She removed the mystique of the kitchen and taught us practicalities – how to separate eggs, melt chocolate, or test a cake to see whether it was ready to remove from the oven. She was strict and taught respect for the knives and the hot hobs, but she also had the patience needed to teach. With her, there was no differentiation between boys and girls. We all could bake basic recipes by the time we were ten, although none of us still can match her soda bread.

We did acquire a small electric ice cream machine and made a number of batches at home, but ice cream at the time was going through an exciting stage in America. Seán and I both remember the first cartons of super-premium ice cream that my mother purchased – tubs of honey vanilla and then coffee. The ingredients were as simple as could be, and none of us could quite believe how thick and dense it was, with a strong custard taste and clarity of flavour. Not all super-premiums survived. A company that made amazing sorbets that none of us will ever forget came and went. Then ice cream with mix-ins

arrived – a catharsis for Seán, who was always crazy for lots of crunchy surprises in his desserts.

On top of the ice cream eating at home, Seán and I were lucky enough to travel a fair bit growing up, accompanying our parents on business trips. We tasted ice creams in many countries and knew what we liked and what we didn't, which ice cream impressed and which disappointed. That knowledge is perhaps the most important part of being in the food business – with strong preferences and confidence in knowing what tastes wonderful, you can figure out (sooner or later) how to make your product a reality. When we decided to open Murphys Ice Cream, Seán enrolled in the ice cream making course at Penn State University. He says he learned more, however, churning ice cream with our small domestic ice cream machine at home, under the watchful eyes of our Aunt Carol. From those small batches to batches for our shops was a relatively small step.

West Kerry – Why?

When I first drove into Dingle in 1990, I was on a trip to Ireland with my mother. There was no question it was beautiful – a whisper of fog on the bay, the brightly painted shops and houses, the mountains rising behind the town into low-lying clouds – yet I had visited beautiful places before. I had no inkling that I would ever live here. A year later, we found ourselves in Ireland again to visit my grandmother and other relations in Cork, and again we drove around the coast and ended up spending a day or two in Dingle. A pint and some music at O'Flaherty's with the murmur of spoken Irish, a tour around Slea Head, a walk on Ventry beach, and we were off again.

Yet Dingle has a way of reeling in people. Within two years I was back – this time with instructions from my parents to look for a house for their retirement, and sure enough I found one. Then I returned to spend a bit of time on a career break, squatting in the newly-purchased house for a month, I thought, or maybe two. That's when West Kerry really worked its magic. I found the locals open and welcoming and the 'blow-ins' interesting. For a town so small, there always seemed to be something happening – a top classical musician, a once-a-year pottery firing over a wood fire in a hand-made kiln, or a Mass at a holy well during the summer solstice. After three months, I headed back to the US and found myself missing Dingle. I worked a few months freelance, then packed up all my belongings and bought a one-way plane ticket.

Seán moved over for slightly different reasons. Not only did he want to start an ice cream company, but he had met his future wife, Wiebke, and Dingle seemed the perfect place to start a family. So it has proved. Their son Conor and daughter Úna can play on the beach, run in the grass with Ivan the dog, and live in a safe and caring environment. They have no shortage of doting relations. Their grandparents retired and moved back to Ireland as planned, and their grandaunt, Carol, has joined us as well.

So now the only hold-out is our sister Deirdre, who lives in Germany. I wouldn't be too surprised if she showed up one day with her family and all her worldly possessions, for West Kerry has a gentle magnetic effect on people. It's kind of sneaky. Like myself, people arrive into town for the first time because they heard about the scenery, but by the second, third, or fourth time, they end up wondering how they could make a life here. Some do, some don't, and some move here and move away again. For us, however, the magnetism is still at work. We might travel in search of sun or the excitement of a city, but each time we return from a trip, drive over Conor Pass and see Dingle laid out before us in all its beauty, we have come home.

'Tourists'
and The Murphys
Laboratory

Of course, Dingle has done more for us than provide good friends and a beautiful and culturally-interesting place to live. It has provided a means for us to stay here. County Kerry is best-known for tourism and football, and while the latter provides great entertainment and conversation, the former provides the bulk of the indigenous employment. Visitors come from all around Ireland and the world for the landscape and 'craic,' and they make a great number of businesses viable, supplementing the local clientele.

We realised early on that huge numbers of tourists return regularly to Kerry. In fact, its hard to even consider them tourists, because so many come at least once a year and more often multiple times a year. This is especially true of the Irish, but it holds for foreign nationals as well. We learned very quickly to welcome everyone who enters our shop as potential life-long customers. This is vital, since the Kerry connections are often surprising. The German 'tourist' might live and work in Inch, the English family could well spend each summer in their grand-parent's cottage in Brandon, the Malaysian could be a doctor in Tralee and the American a visiting professor in Limerick. All share a love for Kerry (as well as ice cream), and we're always delighted to see them again.

Many of our customers have been visiting us since the early days in Dingle, when the proximity of the kitchen in the back of the shop gave us an amazing testing laboratory. Ice cream, coffee and dessert ideas flowed from the kitchen to the front and back again. Seán and I cooked up new recipes, brought them out for trial, and our customers praised the successes and politely sympathised with the failures. We could make a new flavour and know within a day or two whether it was a hit. Likewise, a customer could suggest something, and we could produce it for them to try. Our ice creams, coffees and desserts have been refined over years of conversation between our customers and our kitchen.

Due to our growth, our kitchen is now in a production facility on the edge of Dingle town. The conversation with our customers continues, however, in both our Dingle and Killarney shops. Preferences vary, but when you hear the views of thousands of people over the course of a season, you have a pretty good idea what works and what needs to be changed. Seán and I consider ourselves extremely lucky in terms of our customers. Their breadth of know-ledge, understanding of our vision, and ability to share in our excitement has not only rewarded us personally but has helped us move our business forward. Without their encouragement and persistence, there would be no Murphys Ice Cream as it is today, and all of the following recipes bear their mark.

The Next Step

The first years of Murphys Ice Cream were both extremely exciting and incredibly hard work. Sometimes, in the midst of the long hours, in the shop and the kitchen, in the happy chaos of high season, Seán and I would feel a surge of pride. We had spent so long improving the products we served, and now, almost daily, customers would tell us that they had never tasted ice cream so good. They complimented our coffees as well (especially the Italians), and Seán's wife Wiebke had her own fan club for her German cakes. And yet, there was a point upon which the Irish customers kept complaining.

'Why,' they asked us, 'can't we buy your ice cream in Dublin/Cork/Limerick/Galway?'

Seán, by now, had gravitated toward the front of the shop, and I to the kitchen and to spending more time with the recipes. As I cooked and tinkered, Seán listened to suggestions about where our ice cream might sell and wrote down a list of shops. We had some doubts. We were quite expensive, and therefore our appeal was bound to be limited. Eventually, however, we decided to give it a go.

We filled our most popular ice creams into soup cartons (they were insulated, after all, and we could buy as few of them as we wanted), printed labels off the computer, and tried them out in our local supermarkets – Garvey's and Sheehy's – over the winter of 2003. They sold well, and the following spring, Seán and I climbed into our van and drove to Dublin.

As we drove, we tried to come up with a sales pitch. We could give them a taste, we thought, and we had brought a few dozen samples. We could tell them about the fresh cream and all the care we put into the product. The more we drove, however, the more difficult it seemed to explain why they should stock ice cream from a small shop in Kerry, so we stopped thinking about it. We drove into the 'Big Smoke' in relative silence.

The same shop names had come up again and again among our customers, and Morton's in Ranelagh was at the top of Seán's list. After getting a bit lost, we found it. I stayed with the van, and Seán courageously went in. Within two minutes he was back out again, and my heart sank. Seán was smiling, though, and explained that he didn't get very far with his sales pitch. He found the owner, told him who he was, and was told, 'Fine! Bring it in!'

We packed half of our sample tubs into Morton's freezer, and drove to the next shop, Fothergill's in Rathmines, where we had a similar reception. They took the other half of our samples, and that was the end of our sales calls. Our customers certainly had been right. Within an hour in Dublin, we had ran out of tubs, so we turned around and drove back to Dingle.

It seemed pretty clear that our lives were about to change, and Seán would be spending quite a bit of time on the road. I was thinking about how I needed to get in a much bigger stack of soup containers and labels, and wondering how we would manage to fill all of them. We weren't worrying too much about the practicalities, however. We both knew we had taken a huge step. Within that short trip, Murphys Ice Cream had burst the bounds of County Kerry and was now a national company!

Killarney Comes Calling

As the tub sales increased, and restaurants began serving our ice cream, we started looking for possible towns to open a second shop. Killarney made the most sense, given its proximity to Dingle, but we struggled to find a premises we liked. It was our customers again who helped us when the perfect place came up in the very centre of town. An estate agent, who regularly visited our Dingle shop, had a chance conversation with the landlord. A few phone calls later, a visit or two to a solicitor, and we took possession. We brought out our paint brushes again, and with the help of our plumber, electrician, and refrigeration man, Murphys Ice Cream opened at Main Street Killarney on St. Patrick's Day 2004.

Along with the magnificence of the national park and the lakes, there is a friendliness in Killarney that makes it a joyful place to have a shop. The town also has great civic spirit. There's a reason Killarney has won 'Tidy Town' and other awards – the locals work as one to improve it every year. From the impressive Christmas festivities to the flowers on the streets and shops, Killarney looks well and feels even better. When we opened, virtually all of the shopkeepers along the street came by personally to welcome us and wish us well. Seán and I will never forget that experience.

There is nothing I like better now than to drop into our shop in Killarney. Driving in on an evening, the golden sunlight plays across the mountains, and inside the town, Main Street is bound to be bustling. Then, there it is – the glow from our shop and the music pouring out the open door. I like to stand outside for a few minutes, watching people emerge holding a cone as if it were the most precious thing on earth. Then I enter, and when I see the smiling faces behind the counter, the cappuccino machine steaming away, and the contented customers chatting over ice cream, I think 'This is it.' This is what Seán and I dreamed about when we first opened. This is what we love.

Ingredients and Equipment

I have written about the importance of using good quality ingredients and hope you make the extra effort to find the very best you can.

You will be rewarded amply, for although ice cream is extremely unforgiving in terms of off-flavours, it also brings out the very best when you are using quality.

You might not notice the difference between good and fantastic chocolate in a chocolate cake, but you will very likely taste it in the ice cream.

There are ways to cover inferior ingredients with lots of flavourings or complex combinations that overwhelm the palate, but why bother?

Use a ripe, delicious banana, and you will find you need little else to make the ice cream taste wonderful. Use great chocolate, and any chocaholics in the family will exult. Use great vanilla, and you will know why this flavour endures.

These days, time seems to be our most precious commodity, so if you're going to take the time to make a recipe, don't skimp on the ingredients!

Good places to search for ingredients include:

- Your local farmers or farmer's market for fruit.
- Your local whole food shop for vanilla, spices, Fairtrade coffee and tea, organic chocolate and organic cocoa.
- Your local gourmet shop for gourmet chocolate and other tasty ingredients.

If you can't find what you want, don't be shy! Ask your local shops to bring them in for you. Many will be happy to do so.

The Kerry Cow

When West Kerry farmer Colm Murphy first brought some Kerry cow milk to Murphys Ice Cream for us to sample, we were delighted. The ice cream came out smoother, creamier, and just plain delicious.

The indigenous Kerry cow is one of the oldest breeds in Europe and the first developed for milking. Our ancestors churned Kerry cow butter, made Kerry cow cheeses, and stored milk treated with herbs in jars underground. So valuable was the Kerry that under Brehon Law the top unit of currency was the milking cow, and that cow would have likely been a Kerry.

Ingredient Checklist

- Fresh cream. Outside of Ireland, use heavy cream or whipping cream. Here in Ireland, your local cream should be perfectly delicious as long as it is really fresh. Do not use UHT (long-life) cream.
- Fresh milk. Enough said.
- Good quality, fresh eggs. We use free range eggs, and the flavour is much better than the ordinary ones. Organic would be better again.
- Fresh, ripe fruit. If you can't find it out of season, wait for the season to come and make something else! Fruit that is not ripe will be quite tasteless.
- Real flavours – when looking for vanilla, almond, etc., get the real thing! If in doubt, read the label.
- Top quality, high cocoa content chocolate. Normally we use 70%. If you use low cocoa content chocolate, you will be adding a lot of fat and losing flavour.

Food Safety and Pasteurisation

As always, in the kitchen, pay attention to basic food safety. Keep a clean kitchen, use fresh ingredients, and you should be fine.

It is, however, important to state that many of the recipes in here call for eggs, and care is required. We will include instructions on pasteurisation with every ice cream recipe that contains eggs, and this is a must for pregnant women.

In all other cases, whether you pasteurise or not is up to you, and should really be a function of whether

you trust the ingredients you use and the suppliers who supplied them.

If in doubt, pasteurise!

Pasteurisation is simply a matter of using temperature (i.e. cooking) to kill bacteria, and if you do decide to pasteurise, a good thermometer is critical. There is very little leeway between keeping the custard hot enough and in scrambling the eggs, which will give you solid bits and an over-cooked taste. Basically you would want to bring the ice cream mix to 73C, maintaining the custard at that temperature for at least five minutes, stirring continuously. Be careful! If the custard rises much above 76C, you will cook the eggs!

If you do over-cook the mix but still want to use it, you could pass it through a strainer to remove any bits and pieces, but it could well change the final product.

For more on food safety, visit www.fsai.ie – the Food Safety Authority of Ireland's website.

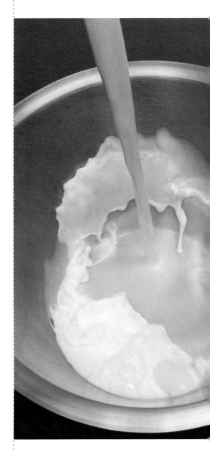

You may not know:

The frozen base of a passive ice cream machine is also great for serving ice cubes at a cocktail party (it will keep them from melting) or for keeping a wine bottle cool at the dinner table (chill it, fill it with water, and it works like an ice bucket).

A Quick Safety List

- Make sure you wash your hands before handling food and after breaking eggs and discarding the shells.
- Ensure your ingredients are fresh and within their sell-by or best-before dates.
- The safe range for your refrigerator is between 1–5C.
- Keep raw, potentially dangerous items such as meat on the lowest shelves of the refrigerator so that they don't drip on and contaminate other items.
- Don't re-freeze anything that has completely thawed, including ice cream!

- Measuring cups.
- A kitchen scale.
- An electric mixer or a whisk if you're energetic!
- A mixing bowl.
- A thick-bottomed sauce pan. A thick bottom disperses heat more evenly and makes it less likely anything will burn.
- A wooden or heat-safe plastic spoon for stirring.
- A thermometer if you want to pasteurise the mix.
- A double boiler if you're melting chocolate, although you can use a microwave.
- A sieve.
- A blender or food processor.
- Freezer-proof containers for storing the ice cream.

What equipment you might need and want:

While it is possible to make ice cream by simply putting the mix in the freezer and stirring it every few hours, we definitely suggest investing in a domestic ice cream machine, and it need not be expensive. The improvement in consistency will be immense. The reason for this is that the different components in ice cream (fat, water, etc.) freeze quite quickly. That means the ice cream tends to separate as it freezes, and you can be left with icy bits in the final product. A machine will stir the mix while it is freezing, keeping it from separating and making it much less likely that iciness will occur.

There are two types of domestic ice cream machines – passive and active. The first has a base that you stick in the freezer a day before you want it, then pull out to use. The second has a freezer unit built in. The advantage of the first is cost – it is usually a quarter of the cost. The disadvantage of a passive unit is that it has to be chilled before you can make ice cream, whereas with an active unit, it's ready to go at an instant's notice. The second advantage is that you can make back to back batches, since a passive unit will need to be re-frozen each time.

There really won't be any difference in the quality of the final produce with either machine. It's just a matter of convenience. How much ice cream are you going to make? For most people, an inexpensive, passive ice cream maker will be perfectly suitable for all your ice cream needs.

Units and Measures

For the purpose of this cookbook, we will use almost exclusively metric measures. The main reason for this is to avoid confusion. A cup is not necessarily a cup – in the UK a cup (Imperial) is 10 oz, whereas in the US a cup is 8 oz. What makes this more confusing is that depending on the manufacturer of the cup, you could easily find yourself buying a US measuring cup in the UK or Ireland. The difference is 20 per cent, which is huge in terms of the final product. We drove ourselves crazy in the early days trying to figure out why recipes would come out so differently, and it turned out to be a function simply of which measuring cup we happened to pick up! The one exception to our metric rule is teaspoons and tablespoons, but even then, we will usually give the metric equivalent.

WEIGH YOUR DRY AND SOLID INGREDIENTS!

Due to variations in the final product, we started weighing all of our dry ingredients, and we suggest you do the same. A basic kitchen scale is a very cheap investment that will pay huge dividends. This is because a cup of sugar, for example, depending on how packed it is, can easily make ice cream too sweet. You might give the sugar in the measuring cup a little shake to level it for an easier reading, and that shake settles the sugar. That means you will need more to fill the cup, and the ice cream will turn out sweeter. All of this goes away when weighing it. Other dry or solid ingredients have similar issues – for example, I've never known how to pack butter into a cup! Also, what's a cup of chocolate? You can buy chocolate as a bar, little drops, or big pieces, and each will fill a cup differently. So the easiest thing is to use weight!

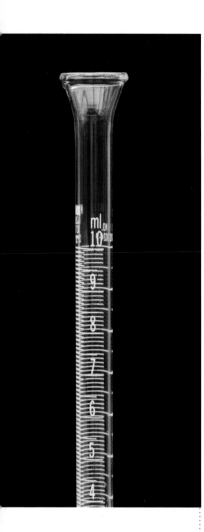

Conversions

If my arguments above didn't convince you, and you don't want to go metric, here's a little bit of help with conversions. If you find it too confusing, double check your measuring cup. The millilitres should be on there!

The easiest way to convert from metric is to go online, where there are numerous conversion sites and handy conversion tools …

LIQUID MEASURES

To get a US cup, divide the number of millilitres by 236. To get a UK cup, divide the millilitres by 284. So, for example, 200 ml would be .7 of a UK cup.

If it's helpful, there are 29.5 ml in a US fluid ounce, and 28.4 ml in a UK fluid ounce.

Check your cup! If there are 10 fl. oz. in a cup, it's UK, and if there are 8 fl. oz, it's US.

Ml	Cup (US)	Cup (UK)	Fl. Oz (US)	Fl. Oz (UK)
100	.423	.352	3.38	3.52
200	.847	.704	6.76	7.04

WEIGHT

28.35g = 1 oz, so divide the number of grams by 28.35 to get the number of ounces.

Gram	Ounce (avdp)
100	3.53
200	7.06

TEMPERATURE

Here's a really confusing one – to get Fahrenheit from Celsius, take the temperature in Celsius, divide by 5, multiply by 9, and add 32.

Stated mathematically, it's $[°F] = [°C] \times 9/5 + 32$

CELSIUS	FAHRENHEIT	
-18	0.4	Your freezer should be at least this cold
-12	10.4	Ice cream temperature perfect for serving
0	32	Water freezes
1-5	33.8-41	Refrigeration temperature
10.6	51.1	Average yearly temperature in Kerry
20	68	Temperature we wish it was in Kerry
37	98.6	Body temperature and chocolate melting point
73	163	Pasteurisation temperature that we will be using
100	212	Water boils
115	239	Use this for making fudge (soft ball stage)
125	257	Candy temperature (hard ball stage)
180	356	Popular baking temperature
6000	10832	Temperature on the sun

Buying, Storing, and Making Ice Cream

BUYING ICE CREAM

You might be exclusively making your own ice cream from now on, but I thought it might be helpful to pass on a few tips for buying it – just in case.

Ice cream can become icy or grainy when it's not stored properly and flavours can taste diminished. The main culprit for this is temperature fluctuations, whether during transport, storage, or simply from taking it out and putting it back in the freezer. If ice cream is not stored cold enough, the quality will also suffer.

So, when you're at the shop:

1. Do the rest of your shopping first and pick up the ice cream last.
2. Make sure the ice cream is well within its 'best before' date.
3. Make sure the ice cream is hard in the freezer. If a tub feels soft, the shop's display freezer is probably

not cold enough and the ice cream may not be at its best. If it's a regular occurrence, you should definitely bring it to the attention of the shop manager. (If it's a tub of Murphys Ice Cream, please email us as well!)

4. If the ice cream is soft, it will melt even faster, so don't dawdle!

5. If you know the ice cream will be out of the freezer for a good while, you might choose chocolate ice cream or a sorbet, which are generally more robust and melt slower. Flavours with alcohol will melt quicker.

6. Fully natural ice creams like our own will be more delicate and dislike temperature fluctuations more than ice creams that are very stabilised.

STORING ICE CREAM

It's important that you store ice cream properly.

1. Whether you've just made it or just bought some, don't let ice cream sit on the counter! Freeze it immediately!

2. This is especially true when returning from a shopping trip. Put the ice cream in the freezer first (that is, if you don't want to eat it immediately), before all other frozen goods. The reason for this is that most ice creams will be soupy at -10C, while most other frozen foods will still be, well, frozen.

3. Bury it in the back of the freezer, if possible. Each time you open the freezer door, you are letting in warm air. The further away from the door it is, the better.

4. Store your ice cream as cold as possible. If you have a freezer that is colder (chest freezers are usually around -30C if turned all the way up) and one that is warmer (a normal freezer should be at least -18C), keep it in the cold one!

5. If you open it, eat some, and wish to return it to

the freezer, put a layer of plastic wrap over the tub before replacing the lid. It will help keep the ice cream air-tight.

6. Finally, never refreeze ice cream that has been out of the freezer a long time or has melted! It could be a food safety issue.

SOME TIPS ON MAKING ICE CREAM

I have tried to be as specific as possible with the recipes, but here are a few tips that might help:

1. Read the section on ingredients!
2. Ingredients vary, and the ice cream might not come out the same for you as for someone else. If this is the case, don't be afraid to tinker with the recipes. You might also wish to do so to suit your tastes. However, you should know that good consistency in natural ice cream is due to a balance of solids, fat, and liquid. Changing ingredients might well change the consistency. Generally:
3. If the ice cream comes out coarse or icy, either add more fat (cream) or solids (sugar or egg yolks) or reduce the liquid (milk, or water in sorbet). Adding a bit of alcohol will likely help as well.
4. If the ice cream comes out soggy, either reduce the fat (cream) or solids (sugar or egg yolks) or increase the liquid (milk, or water in sorbet). You can also reduce alcohol if the recipe contains it.
5. Always make sure the mix going into the ice cream machine is cold or it might not freeze properly.
6. Any mix-ins such as cookies should be added to the ice cream mix only when the ice cream is semi-frozen. Otherwise, they will sink to the bottom.

Once you can successfully make the custard base, you can make ice cream. Here's some extra detail to supplement the recipes:

1. It's easier to separate eggs when they are at room temperature, so it might be a good idea to leave them out for half an hour or so before you begin.

2. Beating the sugar and egg yolks together is important, since it protects the eggs from heat shock when exposed to the hot milk.

3. Pouring the milk into the egg and sugar mixture slowly, stirring all the time, will lessen the shock.

4. Pans generally distribute heat unevenly, so it's important to stir the custard, or it might stick around the edges. Stirring it will also distribute the temperature evenly throughout the cooking custard.

5. If you have trouble keeping the custard from overheating, you could use a double boiler, although it will take longer.

6. The custard won't thicken as much as other custards, but it will thicken slightly and should lightly coat the back of a spoon.

7. When whipping the cream, don't over-whip! It should double in volume and create soft peaks. The reason to do this is to make the ice cream fluffier. If you like a richer ice cream, you could use the same amount of cream without whipping it.

8. I use the term 'fold' to mean 'gently combine the cream and custard.' A way to do this is to stir in from the side of the bowl, down to the bottom centre and then up to the top centre, rotating the bowl as you do so. The reason you need to refrain from over-mixing is that you can stir the air out of the whipped cream, which defeats the purpose of whipping it.

Basic Ice Cream Recipes

For Seán and I, these are the core flavours. The simplest ice creams are not necessarily the easiest to make, so perhaps they shouldn't be called 'basic.' Still, these are a great starting point, and many of them can be altered to fit your own preferences. Whether it's adding bits of candy bar to the vanilla ice cream or dropping a splash of cognac in the chocolate, feel free to play!

Note: We have given almost all of our ice creams Irish names. They are not always literal. You will find them in parenthesis after the English name.

BANANA (BANANA) ICE CREAM WITH CHOCOLATE SHAVINGS

For some of us who eat bananas regularly, we do so hardly noticing how they taste, not really paying attention to why they are such an incredibly popular fruit. Put them in ice cream, however, and you will rediscover bananas as one of the most marvellous gifts of nature. It is not always easy to find ripe bananas in these parts, and most of the time I will pass them by when in the supermarket, discouraged at the green peel. Just one look, and I know that they will be hard and, chemically speaking, a different fruit altogether. For, as bananas ripen, the starches turn to sugar, and once they do so, this sweet, complex, rich, and velvety fruit can boost energy and give any occasion a lift.

1. All fruits in ice cream should be ripe, and with bananas there is hardly such a thing as too ripe. If you have bananas left over with brown spots on the skin, perhaps ones that the kids won't touch or that even strike you as too soft, then they are perfect for ice cream. We have used bananas when the skin had turned completely brown, and the result was delicious. Bananas, oddly enough, ripen best off the vine, and if all you have is green bananas, please wait to make this ice cream and let them ripen.

You may not know:

As well as a fruit, bananas have a flower that is enjoyed raw or cooked in curries and soups in Southeast Asia.

Ingredients:

- 130g sugar
- 5 egg yolks
- 240ml cream
- 200ml milk
- 15ml (1 tablespoon) fresh lemon juice
- 3 ripe bananas
- 20g good quality, dark chocolate

What to do:

1. Combine the bananas with the lemon juice and blend or mash until smooth.

2. Place in a small saucepan, add 30g (two tablespoons) sugar, and cook over low heat, stirring all the time.

3. Don't over-cook. Once it has warmed, it should release a strong banana aroma, and that's enough!

4. Beat the rest of the sugar and egg yolks together until thick and pale yellow.

5. Bring the milk to a low simmer in a small sauce-

pan. Remove from the heat.

6. Beat the milk into the eggs and sugar in a slow stream.

7. Pour the mixture back into the pan and place over low heat.

8. Stir continuously until the custard thickens slightly (around 65–70C) and just coats the back of a spoon. Don't over-heat, though, because at around 76C you will scramble the eggs!

9. Immediately remove from the heat.

10. Mix in the bananas.

11. Transfer the custard into a small container, cover, and refrigerate until cool (5C).

12. Whip the cream until it has doubled in volume (you should have soft peaks – don't over-whip).

13. Fold the cream (gently stir) into the custard.

14. Freeze using a domestic ice cream machine until it has a semi-solid consistency, or cover and place in the freezer, stirring occasionally to break up the ice crystals.

15. Use a vegetable peeler to create the chocolate

Seán's Favourite Pairing:

Bananas go really well with walnuts, so you could serve this with a waffle or crêpe topped with a few walnuts and a splash of caramel sauce.

Recipe continues ...

shavings, and add them to the ice cream once it is reasonably solid, or they will all sink to the bottom.

16. If you're using a domestic ice cream machine, transfer to a freezer-proof covered container when the ice cream has achieved a semi-solid consistency (around 15 minutes). Place it in the freezer, and continue to freeze until it is solid.

Yield: 8 servings

Notes:

o   You don't have to add chocolate shavings if it's not to your taste, but I love the combination of banana and the bitterness of the chocolate.

o   To pasteurise the eggs, heat the custard to 73C and maintain that temperature for at least 5 minutes. Use a cooking thermometer, and keep stirring! If the custard goes any higher than 76C, the eggs will scramble. Immediately cover and place in the freezer until cool.

CHOCOLATE (SECLÁID) ICE CREAM

I love chocolate! There really isn't much more to say about my feelings for that luscious substance, and what could be better than chocolate ice cream? Chocolate originated in Central America as a drink enhanced with chilli peppers and other spices. Made by crushing the cocoa plant's seeds, it was revered in ancient Mayan culture and was integral to religious and royal ceremonies. Later, the Aztecs grew to love it, and chocolate became a huge part of their economy. It was so precious, that they used cocoa beans as currency. In Aztec mythology, the first cocoa tree came from paradise, carried down on the beam of the morning star by the god Quetzalcoatl.

Chocolate was one of the very first ice creams we made, and it remains our second best seller, behind honeycomb. However, if you combined our different chocolate flavours, chocolate would outsell everything else by far! This chocolate ice cream is dense, creamy, and smooth. It's designed to lift you up, romance a loved one, or put a smile on anybody's face. It's not so strong to put off the faint-hearted, but neither should it leave a chocaholic disappointed. That being said, it's hard to get the balance of chocolate right, and of course people's preferences vary wildly on this subject. Seán and I spent a lot of time working on our chocolate ice cream. We have tested, tasted, debated, re-tasted, argued, and tested again until we found ourselves pleased.

It is important to note when you're making chocolate ice cream that the chocolate you use will have a huge bearing on the final result. Definitely use top quality dark chocolate. Which one is up to you, and you might want to experiment with different brands to get the best result. We actually use a combination of two chocolates – one quite sharp, the other deep and full-flavoured. We have used very expensive single estate chocolates on occasion, and you certainly will notice the difference if you want to treat yourself or your guests …

You may not know:

Chocolate was simply a drink until relatively recently. It was 1857 before British chocolatier J.S. Frey invented the solid chocolate bar.

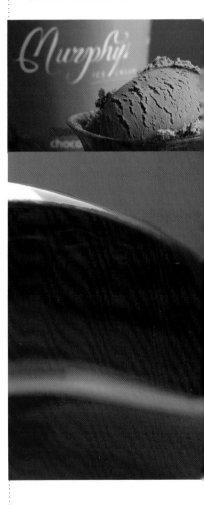

Ingredients:

- 100g sugar
- 4 egg yolks
- 220ml milk
- 200ml cream
- 150g dark (70%) chocolate
- 1/4 teaspoon pure vanilla extract

A tip from our kitchen:

When melting chocolate, the pot or pan must be completely dry, or the chocolate will clump!

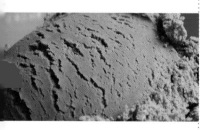

Seán's Favourite Pairing:

Chocolate sauce, chocolate cake, chocolate shavings and whipped cream. How can you have enough chocolate? We serve the above combination in the shops for chocaholics in dire need of a fix.

WHAT TO DO:

1. Melt the chocolate in a double boiler over simmering water or in a microwave. Take care – chocolate melts at a low temperature (approx. 37C) and it burns easily!

2. Beat the sugar and egg yolks together until pale yellow.

3. Bring the milk to a low simmer.

4. Remove from the heat and beat the milk into the egg and sugar mixture in a slow stream. Pour the mixture back into the pan and place over low heat.

5. Stir continuously until the custard thickens slightly (around 65–70C) and just coats the back of a spoon. Don't over-heat, though, because at around 76C you will scramble the eggs! Immediately remove from the heat.

6. Add to the melted chocolate in small parts and mix thoroughly until smooth and velvety.

7. Cover the chocolate custard with plastic wrap and refrigerate until cool.

8. Stir in the vanilla. Whip the cream until it has doubled in volume (you should have soft peaks – don't over-whip).

9. Fold the cream (gently stir) into the custard.

10. Freeze using a domestic ice cream machine, or cover and place in the freezer, stirring every few hours to break up the ice crystals.

11. If you're using a domestic ice cream machine, transfer to a freezer-proof covered container when the ice cream has achieved a semi-solid consistency (around 15 minutes). Place it in the freezer, and continue to freeze until it is solid.

Yield: 8 servings

Notes:

o   The chocolate and the custard must both be

warm when you mix them or you won't get a good emulsion.

o   To pasteurise the eggs, heat the custard to 73C and maintain that temperature for at least 5 minutes. Use a cooking thermometer, though! If the custard goes any higher than 76C, the eggs will scramble. Immediately cover and place in the freezer until cool.

CINNAMON (CAINÉAL) ICE CREAM

I have decked my bed with coverings of tapestry, with carved works, with linen from Egypt. I have perfumed my bed with myrrh, aloes, and cinnamon. Come, let us take our fill of love until the morning.

– Proverbs 7:17-18

Cinnamon is a spice valued from earliest antiquity. A small evergreen tree native to Sri Lanka and India, its precious bark was used by the early Egyptians, in Roman funeral pyres, and was considered a gift worthy of a king. The source of the spice remained a closely guarded secret, however. Arab traders carried it overland to Alexandria in the Middle Ages, where Venetians bought it and distributed it to Europe. It took until the fifteenth century for the Portuguese to discover what was then known as Ceylon, although they were subsequently ousted by the Dutch who in turn lost out to the British. Of course none of this really concerns us, but a taste of cinnamon can make almost anyone understand its value.

Whether on a cappuccino or French toast, in an apple pie or in ice cream, cinnamon is a warming spice, perfect for the colder days of autumn and winter. Even in ice cream, it warms the body and soul. Of the many ice creams that we make, Cinnamon is definitely one of the 'Oh my God' flavours. It might not appeal to everyone, but there are so many (including Seán's son,

You may not know:

The word 'cinnamon' comes via Hebrew and Greek from the Malay word, 'kayu manis' meaning 'sweet wood.'

Conor) who not only like this flavour – they absolutely adore it. In fact, it seems to come up out of all proportion when people talk about the best ice cream they have ever tasted. Maybe there was a reason they kept this spice a secret, for it does indeed seem to win people's hearts. Great on its own, especially after a heavy meal, it is also perfectly suited to accompany other desserts, especially those made with fruits. It's also heavenly in an Affogato (see 'Ice Cream Desserts').

Ingredients:

- 130g sugar
- 5 egg yolks
- 240ml cream
- 200ml milk
- 1 cinnamon stick (see note below)

A tip from our kitchen:

You can re-use the cinnamon stick, but make sure you rinse it carefully and let it dry!

WHAT TO DO:

1. Put the cinnamon stick in a saucepan with the milk.
2. Bring the milk to a low simmer.
3. Remove from the heat.
4. Beat the sugar and egg yolks together until thick and pale yellow.
5. Remove the cinnamon stick from the milk.
6. Beat the milk into the eggs and sugar in a slow stream.
7. Pour the mixture back into the pan, and place over low heat.
8. If you want a strong cinnamon flavour, add the cinnamon stick back in.
9. Stir continuously until the custard thickens slightly (around 65–70C) and just coats the back of a spoon. Don't over-heat, though, because at around 76C you will scramble the eggs!
10. Immediately remove from the heat.
11. Remove the cinnamon stick.
12. Transfer the custard into a small container, cover, and refrigerate until cool (5C).
13. Whip the cream until it has doubled in volume (you should have soft peaks – don't over-whip).
14. Fold the cream (gently stir) into the custard.
15. Freeze using a domestic ice cream machine, or cover and place in the freezer, stirring every few hours to break up the ice crystals.

16. If you're using a domestic ice cream machine, transfer to a freezer-proof covered container when the ice cream has achieved a semi-solid consistency (around 15 minutes). Place it in the freezer, and continue to freeze until it is solid.

Yield: 8 servings

Notes:

o   You can substitute 1/2 teaspoon ground cinnamon for the stick. If you do so, mix it into the sugar before beating in the eggs.

o   To pasteurise the eggs, heat the custard to 73C and maintain that temperature for at least 5 minutes. Use a cooking thermometer, though! If the custard goes any higher than 76C, the eggs will scramble. Immediately cover and place in the freezer until cool.

COFFEE (CAIFE) ICE CREAM WITH CHOCOLATE SHAVINGS

One might quibble with me that this is hardly a 'basic' flavour, but I wanted to put our 'Caife' ice cream in the front of the book because besides our vanilla ice cream, it's the ice cream of which I am most proud. Coffee ice cream can be quite difficult – the usual way to make it would be to use instant coffee grounds (which I wouldn't touch out of principle) or risk iciness by using enough coffee to have a good flavour. Coffee liqueur helps to keep the ice cream smooth, and the espresso gives a decent kick. Add in the chocolate shavings, and you have my three favourite things – coffee, chocolate, and ice cream. It's a little bit of frozen heaven.

This is not one of our best-selling ice creams (although it has more than its share of devotees), and it is not for the kids. This is a complex, adult ice cream that will impress coffee and ice cream lovers at a dinner party or give a bit of comfort during a weepy movie. If

Seán's favourite Pairing:

It is perfect with a traditional bread and butter pudding.

You may not know:

Coffee is the most popular beverage worldwide, with 400 billion cups consumed a year.

you have kids, put them to bed, pull out the spoons, and enjoy this with the grown-ups as a bit of special time. For me, this is the ice cream I'm most likely to eat when I'm standing at the scooping cabinet. It's the ice cream I'm most likely to hand out if a customer asks me which flavour I like best. The coffee cuts sweetness, the chocolate melts on the palate, and it still transports me after all these years. I can only hope you like it as much as I do!

Ingredients:

- 130g + 1 table-spoon sugar
- 5 egg yolks
- 240ml cream
- 200ml milk
- 125ml espresso
- 45ml (3 tables-poons) Kahlua liqueur
- 20g good quality dark chocolate

WHAT TO DO:

1. Add one tablespoon of the sugar to the espresso and reduce over medium heat until it is about one-third of its volume (40 ml). Cool.

2. Beat the egg yolks into the rest of the sugar until thick and pale yellow.

3. Bring the milk to a low simmer.

4. Slowly beat the milk into the eggs and sugar.

5. Pour the mixture back into the pan and place over low heat.

6. Stir continuously until the custard thickens slightly (around 65–70C) and just coats the back of a spoon. Don't over-heat, though, because at around 76C you will scramble the eggs!

7. Immediately remove from the heat.

8. Cover the custard with plastic wrap and refrigerate until cool to refrigerator temperature (5C).

9. Mix the espresso and Kahlua and stir into the cooled custard.

10. Whip the cream until it has doubled in volume (you should have soft peaks – don't over-whip).

11. Fold the cream (gently stir) into the custard.

12. Use a potato peeler to shave the chocolate, keeping the shavings as long and thin as possible. Stir into the mix.

13. Freeze using a domestic ice cream machine, or cover and place in the freezer, stirring every few hours to break up the ice crystals.

14. If you're using a domestic ice cream machine, transfer to a freezer-proof covered container when the ice cream has achieved a semi-solid consistency (around 15 minutes). Place it in the freezer, and continue to freeze until it is solid.

Yield: 8 servings

Notes

o   Make sure you add the liqueur when the custard is cold or the alcohol will evaporate.

o   To pasteurise the eggs, heat the custard to 73C and maintain that temperature for at least 5 minutes. Use a cooking thermometer, though! If the custard goes any higher than 76C, the eggs will scramble. Immediately cover and place in the freezer until cool.

o   Instead of creating chocolate shavings, you can also melt the chocolate and pour it into the ice cream machine as its turning.

A tip from our kitchen:

If you can't get espresso, you can brew a very dark coffee and reduce it, but you would probably want to start with 500ml coffee and reduce it to around 50ml.

Seán's Favourite Pairing:

You can amplify all of the flavours here by making a dessert with the ice cream, chocolate sauce, and chocolate covered cocoa beans.

COOKIES (BRIOSCAÍ) ICE CREAM

Cookies is a flavour so popular and so beloved by a great portion of our customers, that we dare not change it or remove it from our cabinet. We have tried doing so in the past but had a massive customer revolt. In fact, the displeasure of our cookie-loving clientele is awesome to behold. Although we sometimes question the cookies we use (they are one of only two ingredients that are not fully natural, jaffa cakes being the other), our customers clearly believe that something that tastes so good belongs in our shop. We don't really dare to tell them otherwise.

Besides our customers, we have slightly more selfish reason to keep making this ice cream. The chocolate biscuits with a white centre have an emotional hold on Seán and I since they are so imbued with childhood memories. Besides ice cream, cookies dipped in

milk was a staple diet in our otherwise health food household. They marked those sleepy hours before bedtime, or precious family moments on a rainy day. I know that we're not the only people who have such attachment to biscuits or sweets from childhood, and maybe the boost to the spirit from a furtive snack on them in adulthood outweighs the negatives. Even now, when stressed and working late in production, I've been known to open a pack of them and pour out a glass of the requisite milk. It's very calming, and it doesn't take many cookies to get me back on track.

Many cookies, including the chocolate chip recipe in this book, are marvellous in ice cream for the same reason they are great with milk. Their dryness and crunch are so perfectly suited to a dairy accompaniment. Put in ice cream, they also add a delightful texture that offsets the smoothness. Of course, there are many different brands that you could use and still have a great result. In fact, we would be happy if you played around to see if it worked with your secret biscuit indulgence. The ratio of ingredients should be more or less the same, and we'd only say that you should stick to cookies that are dry, as the gooey ones might well behave in unexpected ways.

Ingredients:

- 130g sugar
- 5 egg yolks
- 240ml cream
- 200ml milk
- ¼ vanilla bean (optional)
- 4 cookies

WHAT TO DO:

1. Cut the vanilla bean lengthwise and put in a saucepan with the milk.
2. Bring the milk to a low simmer.
3. Remove from the heat.
4. Beat the sugar and egg yolks together until thick and pale yellow.
5. Remove the vanilla bean from the milk.
6. Beat the milk into the eggs and sugar in a slow stream.
7. Pour the mixture back into the pan, and place over low heat.
8. Stir continuously until the custard thickens slightly

(around 65–70C) and just coats the back of a spoon. Don't over-heat, though, because at around 76C you will scramble the eggs!

9. Immediately remove from the heat.

10. Transfer the custard into a small container, cover, and refrigerate until cool (5C).

11. Whip the cream until it has doubled in volume (you should have soft peaks – don't over-whip).

12. Fold the cream (gently stir) into the custard.

13. Crush the cookies into small pieces.

14. Freeze using a domestic ice cream machine, adding the cookies when it's fairly solid.

15. You can also just cover and place in the freezer, stirring every few hours, and again, add the cookies when it's reasonably solid.

16. If you're using a domestic ice cream machine, transfer to a freezer-proof covered container when the ice cream has achieved a semi-solid consistency (around 15 minutes). Place it in the freezer, and continue to freeze until it is solid.

Notes:

o The vanilla is optional, but we like a base flavour of vanilla for this ice cream …

o To pasteurise the eggs, heat the custard to 73C and maintain that temperature for at least 5 minutes. Use a cooking thermometer, and keep stirring! If the custard goes any higher than 76C, the eggs will scramble. Immediately cover and place in the freezer until cool.

Seán's Favourite Pairing:

Cookies ice cream makes a fantastic milkshake. Take two scoops, add a bit of milk, put it in the blender, and indulge …

A tip from our kitchen:

The reason not to add the cookies too early, is that they can turn the ice cream an awful grey colour if they get too much mixing!

You may not know:

The very first cookies are thought to have originated in Persia (present-day Iran) in the seventh century AD.

HONEYCOMB CRUNCHY CARAMEL (CARAMAL) ICE CREAM

Anyone in the ice cream business knows that almost anything with caramel in it is bound to be a success. Our Honeycomb Crunchy Caramel is the most popular ice cream in our shops, and in production during the summer months, we can hardly make enough. Sometimes we've even been known to grumble about the New Zealanders who invented it, because it is one of the most labour intensive ice creams we produce. You can't really be grumpy though, because it brings so much pleasure to so many people. Not only does it sell extremely well in our own shops – it's one of our top-selling tubs as well. The combination of a light caramel base with the crunchy bits of honeycomb make it a completely addictive flavour, and perfect for those with a sweet tooth.

Honeycomb ice cream is a perfect accompaniment for many desserts, from tart fruits to sumptuous cakes, and so universally popular that I have included it under 'basic' recipes. It is, however, one of the most challenging flavours to make in this book. There's always something slightly magical for me about caramel – a transformation of sugar through heat into an amber, delicious liquid. You will have to master this process – to make the honeycomb pieces as well as caramel sauce. Both might well require a bit of practise, but don't give up! You should know that even the best of us in our ice cream kitchen burn caramel from time to time! With a bit of patience and a watchful eye, you will have an ice cream that will enthral anyone to whom you feed it. If you make it too well, however, you might end up as in demand as our kitchen in summer!

You may not know:

The amber colour of caramel occurs when the molecules of sucrose break down under intense heat into various simpler sugars.

WHAT TO DO:

1. Make the honeycomb pieces and break them into small bits. You will need 200ml volume, more or less (depending how many bits you like).
2. Once they are broken, shake them in a sieve to remove any powder.
3. Make the caramel sauce.
4. Beat the sugar and egg yolks together until thick and pale yellow.
5. Bring the milk to a low simmer.
6. Beat the milk into the eggs and sugar in a slow stream.
7. Pour the mixture back into the pan, and place over low heat.
8. Stir continuously until the custard thickens slightly (around 65–70C) and just coats the back of a spoon. Don't over-heat, though, because at around 76C you will scramble the eggs!
9. Transfer the custard into a small container, cover, and refrigerate until cool (5C).
10. Whip the cream until it has doubled in volume (you should have soft peaks – don't over-whip).
11. Fold the cream (gently stir) into the custard.
12. Freeze using a domestic ice cream machine, adding the honeycomb pieces and caramel sauce when it's fairly solid.
13. You can also just cover and place in the freezer, stirring every few hours, and again, add the honeycomb and caramel when it's reasonably solid.
14. If you're using a domestic ice cream machine, transfer to a freezer-proof covered container when the ice cream has achieved a semi-solid consistency (around 15 minutes). Place it in the freezer, and continue to freeze until it is solid.

Ingredients:

- 130g sugar
- 5 egg yolks
- 220ml cream
- 200ml milk
- 200ml volume (80g) honeycomb pieces (see recipe under 'Candy')
- 15ml (1 tablespoon) caramel sauce (see recipe under 'Sauce')

A tip from our kitchen:

You will have extra caramel sauce left over, and you can always use it as a topping for the ice cream or to make a caramel sundae.

Recipe continues …

Book of Sweet Things

If you can get some really crunchy ginger biscuits, their spiciness and texture are a perfect match with this ice cream.

Notes:

o   Beware of adding any more caramel sauce or the ice cream will get soggy.

o   The part about adding the honeycomb at the end is important, as you don't want the pieces melting in the ice cream.

o   To pasteurise the eggs, heat the custard to 73C and maintain that temperature for at least 5 minutes. Use a cooking thermometer, though! If the custard goes any higher than 76C, the eggs will scramble. Immediately cover and place in the freezer until cool.

MINT (MISMÍN) ICE CREAM

Mint ice cream is not naturally green, and certainly never is green in our shops! Green mint ice cream contains food colouring.

Mint people are kind of funny. There is no other ice cream for which people will ask and, if we don't have it, turn around and march out the door, refusing to consider another flavour. If you don't have chocolate ice cream, you can almost always get someone to buy Chocolate Love or Chocolate Whiskey. If you don't have strawberry, raspberry will probably do. Not so with mint. Mint people are not a huge percentage of our customers, but they sure are stubborn. They know what they like, and that's it. Mind you, I can understand their point of view. Not only was I a mint person myself as a child, but the refreshing coolness of mint, combined with creamy ice cream and the dark crunch of chocolate, makes it beguiling.

The name comes from 'Menthe,' a nymph turned into a plant by the jealous Greek goddess Persephone, and it does have slightly other-worldly addictive properties. I've already written about my forays into chocolate chip mint as a youngster, standing in the kitchen mesmerised by it, and I still love this flavour dearly. In fact, I like my mint in almost every thing. There's mint growing in my garden, even though I'm not much of a gardener, and on a summer's day I relish a minty treat of some description or a cooling drink made with the fresh leaves. If you have mint in your own garden, pick some for this recipe. If not, buy a bundle of fresh mint. Mint extracts are extremely volatile, difficult to control, and generally too aromatic for the palate, so fresh mint is definitely our recommendation.

WHAT TO DO:

1. Put the mint and the milk in a saucepan and bring to a simmer.
2. Remove from the heat.
3. Beat the sugar and egg yolks together until thick and pale yellow.
4. Beat the milk into the eggs and sugar in a slow stream. Don't worry if bits of mint go in as well.
5. Pour the mixture back into the pan, with the mint still in it, and place over low heat.
6. Stir continuously until the custard thickens slightly (around 65–70C) and just coats the back of a spoon. Don't over-heat, though, because at around 76C you will scramble the eggs!
7. Immediately remove from the heat.
8. Transfer the custard into a small container, cover, and refrigerate until cool (5C).
9. Use a sieve to strain and remove the mint leaves.

Ingredients:

- 130g sugar
- 5 egg yolks
- 240ml cream
- 220ml milk
- 10g fresh mint leaves
- 20g chocolate

A tip from our kitchen:

For the best flavour, use only the mint leaves and discard the stalks.

Recipe continues ...

Seán's Favourite
Pairing:

Perch it on top of a crunchy chocolate biscuit, then pour over your favourite dark chocolate – melted! Eat it as the chocolate hardens.

10. Create chocolate shavings using the chocolate and a grater or vegetable peeler.

11. Whip the cream until it has doubled in volume (you should have soft peaks – don't over-whip).

12. Fold the cream (gently stir) into the custard.

13. Freeze using a domestic ice cream machine, adding the chocolate shavings when it's fairly solid.

14. You can also just cover and place in the freezer, stirring every few hours, and again, add the chocolate shavings when it's reasonably solid.

15. If you're using a domestic ice cream machine, transfer to a freezer-proof covered container when the ice cream has achieved a semi-solid consistency (around 15 minutes). Place it in the freezer, and continue to freeze until it is solid.

Notes:

o   To pasteurise the eggs, heat the custard to 73C and maintain that temperature for at least 5 minutes. Use a cooking thermometer, though! If the custard goes any higher than 76C, the eggs will scramble. Immediately cover and place in the freezer until cool.

o   Instead of creating chocolate shavings, you can also melt the chocolate and pour it into the ice cream machine as its turning.

RUM RAISIN (RISÍNÍ) ICE CREAM

A few years ago, a woman in our Dingle shop asked to see the manager. We were extremely busy, and my brother was out on a sales call. As soon as I had a chance to leave the kettles and vats in the back kitchen, I went out to her. She seemed happy enough, which was a relief, and in fact, she was finishing off her last bit of rum raisin with obvious relish. I greeted her, told her I was one of the owners, and she said, 'I just have to tell you that before I retired, I worked for 25 years in an ice cream factory. I like to think I know as much about ice cream as anybody, but I'm a bit confused. I have never tasted a rum raisin like this one, and I have to know where you found such excellent rum flavouring!' I looked at her and said, 'But it's not flavouring. It's real rum!'

That is the very simple trick to making a good rum raisin ice cream. The rum keeps the raisins soft and moist, even when frozen, and it improves the texture dramatically. Of course, you will need a little bit of advance planning, since you should soak the raisins in the rum over-night so that they give a little rum explosion when you bite into them. I had one customer who told me that when making rum raisin at home, he pierces every raisin with a needle before soaking them to make sure they are positively packed with booze. I greatly admire his dedication.

Rum raisin isn't for everyone. There are just as many people who won't touch it as those who think it's the pinnacle of ice creams. If you're on the fence about it, try it in winter on a cold, dark day. For myself, I gravitate toward ice cream flavours that are a bit deeper and a bit warmer when the frosty weather hits. The alcohol in rum raisin will make the ice cream feel less cold on the palate, and I think it's a perfect flavour to serve at Christmas time.

You may not know:

Sugar-based alcoholic drinks are ancient, but the first distillation of rum took place in the seventeenth century on sugar plantations in the Caribbean, where slaves discovered that molasses could be fermented into alcohol.

A tip from our kitchen:

I know I always go on about good ingredients, but this is one time where you definitely shouldn't use your best rum. We use an inexpensive dark rum, since better rums are too delicate and get lost in this particular ice cream.

Ingredients:

- 130g sugar
- 5 egg yolks
- 240ml cream
- 200ml milk
- 50ml dark rum
- 75g raisins
  or sultanas

Seán's Favourite
Pairing:

I like rum raisin and
cinnamon ice cream
together, especially
in the winter.

WHAT TO DO:

1. Combine the rum and the raisins the night before. Cover and let soak.

2. Beat the sugar and egg yolks together until thick and pale yellow.

3. Bring the milk to a low simmer.

4. Remove from the heat.

5. Beat the milk into the eggs and sugar in a slow stream.

6. Pour the mixture back into the pan and place over low heat.

7. Stir continuously until the custard thickens slightly (around 65–70C) and just coats the back of a spoon. Don't over-heat, though, because at around 76C you will scramble the eggs!

8. Immediately remove from the heat.

9. Cover the custard with plastic wrap and refrigerate until cool to refrigeration temperature.

10. Whip the cream until it has doubled in volume (you should have soft peaks – don't over-whip).

11. Fold the cream (gently stir) into the custard.

12. Stir in any excess rum from the soaked raisins, holding back the raisins.

13. Freeze using a domestic ice cream machine, or cover and place in the freezer, stirring every few hours to break up the ice crystals.

14. Add the raisins once the ice cream has become reasonable solid.

15. If you're using a domestic ice cream machine, transfer to a freezer-proof covered container when the ice cream has achieved a semi-solid consistency (around 15 minutes). Place it in the freezer, and continue to freeze until it is solid.

Yield: 8 servings

Notes:

o It is important to soak the raisins in the rum. Otherwise, the raisins will become icy in the ice cream.

o If you want to cut the soaking process a bit, you can prick the raisins with a pin or needle so that the rum will get inside faster.

o To pasteurise the eggs, heat the custard to 73C and maintain that temperature for at least 5 minutes. Use a cooking thermometer, though, and keep stirring! If the custard goes any higher than 76C, the eggs will scramble. Immediately cover and place in the freezer until cool.

STRAWBERRY (SÚ TALÚN) ICE CREAM

One of the real pleasures of our business has been watching children grow up through the lens of our shop. We're generally a place for adults, but we have always entertained families. In many ways they are our favourite customers, because serving them is so rewarding. There is almost always a sense of occasion, and whether they are marking a birthday, a holiday, or simply a Sunday morning, families enliven the shops and make us feel special. Children experience life with such abundant glee, and so much is new and exciting. Seeing them sitting and savouring ice cream in awed silence brings us all joy, especially perhaps, their parents who can enjoy their own ice creams or coffees in relative peace.

Although strawberry ice cream is a flavour that adults eat quite happily, it's small children with whom it really seems to resonate. It's the pink colour, the delicate flavour and the sweet fruitiness of this particular treat. So many of our little customers choose strawberry as their very first taste of Murphys Ice Cream that it is automatically the first taste that we will offer them. There are, of course, exceptions. Raspberry sor-

You may not know:

It seems the nobility in Shakespeare's time prized their strawberries greatly: 'My Lord of Ely, when I was last in Holburn, I saw good strawberries in your garden there; I do beseech you, send for some of them.' Gloucester, *Richard III*, Act III, Scene iv

Ingredients:

- 130g sugar
- 5 egg yolks
- 240ml cream
- 200ml milk
- 200g fresh strawberries
- 15ml (1 table-spoon) fresh lemon juice
- 1 teaspoon vanilla essence

A tip from our kitchen:

Fruit contains a lot of water and will become icy in ice cream. Cooking fruit with sugar will counter this effect.

bet, with it's deeper pink-red colour and sweet acidity appeals to some, and there are always those little chocaholics. Still, strawberry ice cream has delighted so many children, that we consider it a gateway to Murphys.

We hope that this flavour is as popular in your own home, and that it brings you the special time that so many have found in our shops. It's not a very difficult ice cream to make, although we beg you to find fresh, ripe strawberries. Ireland has an abundance of them in summer, so perhaps it should be saved for those warm days when the kids are off school and need to be entertained. Making ice cream with them might well be just as enjoyable as eating it when it comes out of the freezer.

WHAT TO DO:

1. Rinse and hull the strawberries.

2. Put them in a food processor or blender and pulse two or three times. You don't want a puree here! Just break them up a bit.

3. Combine the strawberries, the lemon juice, and 30g of the sugar a sauce pan and cook over low heat for about 5 minutes until the sugar is dissolved.

4. Bring the milk to a low simmer.

5. Remove from the heat.

6. Beat the rest of the sugar and egg yolks together until thick and pale yellow.

7. Beat the milk into the eggs and sugar in a slow stream. Pour the mixture back into the pan, and place over low heat.

8. Stir continuously until the custard thickens slightly (around 65–70C) and just coats the back of a spoon. Don't over-heat, though, because at around 76C you will scramble the eggs!

9. Immediately remove from the heat.

10. Transfer the custard into a small container, cover, and refrigerate until cool (5C).

11. Stir in the strawberries and the vanilla.

12. Whip the cream until it has doubled in volume (you should have soft peaks – don't over-whip).

13. Fold the cream (gently stir) into the custard.

14. Freeze using a domestic ice cream machine, or cover and place in the freezer, stirring every few hours to break up the ice crystals.

15. If you're using a domestic ice cream machine, transfer to a freezer-proof covered container when the ice cream has achieved a semi-solid consistency (around 15 minutes). Place it in the freezer, and continue to freeze until it is solid.

Notes:

o Vanilla is optional, but we like it as a base flavour for this ice cream …

o To pasteurise the eggs, heat the custard to 73C and maintain that temperature for at least 5 minutes. Use a cooking thermometer, though! If the custard goes any higher than 76C, the eggs will scramble. Immediately cover and place in the freezer until cool.

Seán's favourite Pairing:

Make an ice cream strawberry shortcake. Take a bit of shortcake, a scoop of strawberry ice cream, some chopped, fresh strawberries, and top it off with fresh cream on a warm July or August afternoon.

VANILLA (FANAILE) ICE CREAM

Vanilla ice cream is one of our most popular and most appreciated flavours. In our shops, however, customers often order vanilla ice cream apologetically, half-expecting criticism for being unadventurous. They sometimes get criticism – not from us, of course, but from a spouse or teenage offspring.

'Oh, Dad,' they might say, rolling their eyes. 'We didn't come all the way to Murphys so you could buy the 'plain' one. That's so boring!'

Plain? Boring? Seán and I heartily disagree. Some people think that vanilla is somehow the absence of flavour, but that is not the case at all. The true taste of a pure, natural vanilla graces just about anything or any mood, so why be shy about liking it? In ice cream, vanilla amplifies rather than obscures the custard, and this winning combination ensures its continuing success. The very simplicity makes it shine.

Creating an excellent vanilla ice cream is much more difficult than people might think. Vanilla is either good or it is not, which is why I almost always sample vanilla when I'm traveling and come upon an ice cream shop. When you produce a strong flavour, perhaps you can cover up any inadequacies. With vanilla, you're completely exposed. Of all the ice creams at Murphys, nothing makes us more proud than when people tell us that our vanilla is the best they have ever tasted.

Not only is vanilla ice cream very hard to make, it is also very expensive (assuming you use the real thing). We use four different natural vanillas in our ice cream to get the right balance – two types of bean, and two types of essence. Both of the essences are well over 100 euro a litre – one is 160 euro a litre. It's the most expensive ingredient we use, and vanilla ice cream is one of our costliest flavours. So, stand up for yourself if you like it!

When making vanilla at home, it's not necessary

You may not know:

Vanilla is an exotic, flowering orchid, found originally in Mexico. Plain? I think not.
The name comes from the Spanish word 'vainilla,' meaning 'little pod.'

to use four vanillas. Feel free to experiment if you can get your hands on a good, natural vanilla essence (a whole foods shop might be your best bet). The following recipe, however, calls for a single vanilla bean. Sometimes it's better not to over-complicate!

As I said earlier, any off-flavours will be amplified with vanilla ice cream, so search out the freshest, best ingredients. Now's the time to buy those organic, free-range eggs and splurge on the best cream you can find. You won't get away with using that four day old milk at the back of the fridge, so don't even think about it!

WHAT TO DO:

1. Beat the sugar and egg yolks together until thick and pale yellow.

2. Cut the vanilla bean lengthwise and put in a saucepan with the milk.

3. Bring the milk to a low simmer. Remove from the heat.

4. Remove the vanilla bean.

5. Beat the milk into the eggs and sugar in a slow stream.

6. Pour the mixture back into the pan, add the vanilla bean again, and place over low heat.

7. Stir continuously until the custard thickens slightly (around 65–70C) and just coats the back of a spoon. Don't over-heat, though, because at around 76C you will scramble the eggs!

8. Immediately remove from the heat.

9. Remove the vanilla bean and scrape the seeds from it with a spoon or blunt knife. Stir the seeds into the custard, using a whisk to disperse them evenly.

10. Transfer the custard into a small container, cover, and refrigerate until cool (5C).

11. Mix in the cream, beating for one minute.

Ingredients:

- 130g sugar
- 5 egg yolks
- 240ml cream
- 200ml milk
- ½ vanilla bean

A tip from our kitchen:

A vanilla bean is costly. Re-use it! Rinse it carefully when you're done, let it dry, then puree it with sugar in a blender or food processor. You could also simply put the vanilla bean in a container with sugar and cover it for a more delicate taste (and no black bits). Vanilla sugar tastes great in coffee, on cereal, over fruit or in baked goods.

Recipe continues ...

A warm, tart apple pie or crumble fresh from the oven practically demands vanilla ice cream. The contrasting sensations – warm/cold, sour/sweet, crunchy/creamy – delight the palate and prove that a great dessert doesn't need to be overly elaborate.

12. Freeze using a domestic ice cream machine, or cover and place in the freezer, stirring every few hours to break up the ice crystals.

13. If you're using a domestic ice cream machine, transfer to a freezer-proof covered container when the ice cream has achieved a semi-solid consistency (around 15 minutes). Place it in the freezer, and continue to freeze until it is solid.

Yield: 8 servings

Notes:

o   If you don't have a vanilla bean, or if you want to experiment, you can use high-quality vanilla essence. It's hard to say how much, since different brands and types of essences vary so much. Add it to the cool custard in very small parts until you have the right amount of flavour.

o   To pasteurise the eggs, heat the custard to 72C and keep at that temperature for at least 5 minutes. Use a cooking thermometer, and keep stirring! If the custard goes any higher than 76C, the eggs will scramble. Immediately cover and place in the freezer until cool.

Irish Ice Cream Recipes

These recipes are a taste of Ireland. You might quibble with the inclusion of a couple of them, since the idea or dessert might have originated in the U.K. or elsewhere, but if they are in this section it's because I think they belong, since they are now part of Irish tradition. We hope that in years to come, Irish traditional ice creams are valued world-wide!

BLACKBERRY AND APPLE (SMÉAR DHUBH) ICE CREAM

There's nothing that defines autumn in Ireland for me more than going blackberry picking. Along the hedgerows in West Kerry, the blackberries grow so abundantly that one can fill a container without hardly taking five paces. Everyone seems to have their favourite spots – some secret, some obvious. There's nothing more relaxing, after a busy summer, than picking and eating these wonderful black treasures. I love to go down to Doonsheen on a clear autumn day, where I can admire the view of Bull's Head and beyond to the Iveragh peninsula while I harvest. If there's a friend along, the chatter is soft and measured as our hands pull and twist. If the day is warm, I'll take a swim afterwards and let the sea wash away the purple stains from my hands.

I'm lucky enough to also have apple trees in my back garden, planted by my landlady, that produce the most wonderful fruit – big, red and crunchy in a good year. One needs to find a use for them before the crows arrive for their annual feast, and one can only eat so many. It didn't take much to put apple and blackberry together – those two fruits are made for each other, and I try to make this ice cream every autumn. If you have access to both fruits, here's a recipe that yields a very creamy dessert with all the goodness of Ireland …

WHAT TO DO:

1. Combine the blackberries, lemon juice, and 25g of the sugar in a small saucepan.

2. Cover and cook over low heat for about 20 minutes, checking occasionally to make sure it doesn't dry out (the moisture from the berries should prevent this).

3. Transfer to a food processor or blender and puree.

You may not know:

The blackberry is an aggregate fruit that is composed of many smaller fruits called 'drupes.' Each individual drupe is called a 'drupelet.'

Ingredients:

- 155g sugar
- 5 egg yolks
- 240ml cream
- 200ml milk
- 50ml lemon juice
- 1 apple (a cooking apple works well)
- 250g fresh blackberries

4. Pass through a sieve, using a spoon or spatula to force through the pulp. Discard the seeds.

5. Peel and core the apple, and blend together with the lemon juice and cooked blackberries as soon as you have strained the latter (it's more liquid when hot, which will make things easier). Refrigerate until cool.

6. Beat the remaining sugar and egg yolks together until thick and pale yellow.

7. Bring the milk to a low simmer. Remove from the heat.

8. Beat the milk into the eggs and sugar in a slow stream.

9. Pour the mixture back into the pan and place over low heat.

10. Stir continuously until the custard thickens slightly (around 65–70C) and just coats the back of a spoon. Don't over-heat, though, because at around 76C you will scramble the eggs!

11. Immediately remove from the heat.

12. Transfer the custard into a small container, cover, and refrigerate until cool (5C).

13. Whip the cream until it has doubled in volume (you should have soft peaks – don't over-whip).

14. Fold the cream (gently stir) into the custard.

15. Stir in the blackberry-apple puree.

16. Freeze using a domestic ice cream machine, or cover and place in the freezer, stirring every few hours to break up the ice crystals.

17. If you're using a domestic ice cream machine, transfer to a freezer-proof covered container when the ice cream has achieved a semi-solid consistency (around 15 minutes). Place it in the freezer, and continue to freeze until it is solid.

Yield: 8 servings

A tip from our kitchen:

Always wash fruit before using it, especially if you pick it yourself!

Recipe continues ...

Seán's Favourite
Pairing:

Chances are if
you're making
this ice cream,
you'll have lots
of blackberries.
Celebrate them!
Serve this ice
cream with fresh
blackberries
and cream.

You may not know:

Bread is one of the
oldest prepared
foods, dating back to
the neolithic period.

Notes:

o   You can add a bit of cinnamon or vanilla if it's
     to your taste.

o   You can also just make the first part of the rec-
     ipe and have a lovely blackberry coulis (sauce)
     that you can use as a decorative topping.

o   To pasteurise the eggs, heat the custard to 73C
     and maintain that temperature for at least 5
     minutes. Use a cooking thermometer, though,
     and keep stirring! If the custard goes any high-
     er than 76C, the eggs will scramble. Immedi-
     ately cover and place in the freezer until cool.

BROWN BREAD (ARÁN DONN) ICE CREAM

In West Kerry, people like to claim brown bread ice
cream as a regional specialty, although it seems to
have originated in England during Victorian times.
I'm leaving it as an Irish flavour because even if it is
not Irish by origin, it has become Irish by tradition.
There are people here who talk about their great-
grandmother's brown bread ice cream, and that's
good enough for me! Brown bread ice cream is not
savoury, as some might think. Instead, it's prepared
with caramelised, brown sugar to give it a crunchy,
sweet burst in the mouth. It's a flavour people love in
the shops, and not only the misty-eyed ladies from
the West, for whom it brings back all sorts of pleasant memories. Tourists as well can't seem to get
enough of it.

We had never heard of brown bread ice cream
when we opened, and it took us quite a few tries to
get it right. In the early days, we tried caramelising
the sugar with the brown bread under a broiler, and
we burned many batches. It was also hard to decide
how chewy or how crunchy to make it. Luckily, we
had customers who gave us helpful suggestions,
especially Vera, the chemist from next door. As we

improved it, we'd bring over a tub and await her verdict. Vera has passed on. We miss her, and I always think of her when making this ice cream. She also, by the way, suggested trying it with Irish cream liqueur, which proved extremely popular. You're welcome to add in a tablespoon as well, if it suits your taste.

I've never known anyone to be disappointed with this ice cream, and I'm sure that you will have some happy ice cream eaters on your hands if you try it. You might be surprised how quickly it disappears!

WHAT TO DO:

1. Beat the sugar and egg yolks together until thick and pale yellow.
2. Bring the milk to a low simmer.
3. Beat the milk into the eggs and sugar in a slow stream.
4. Pour the mixture back into the pan and place over low heat.
5. Stir continuously until the custard thickens slightly (around 65–70C) and just coats the back of a spoon. Don't over-heat, though, because at around 76C you will scramble the eggs!
6. Immediately remove from the heat.
7. Transfer the custard into a small container, cover, and refrigerate until cool (5C).
8. Pour the water into a pan, and add the dark brown sugar.
9. Cook over medium-high heat until it is boiling rapidly. Start stirring, and continue until all the sugar crystals have dissolved and it is completely smooth.
10. Remove from the heat and stir the bread crumbs into the melted sugar.
11. Transfer the custard into a small container, cover, and refrigerate until cool (5C).
12. Whip the cream until it has doubled in volume

Ingredients:

- 110g sugar
- 5 egg yolks
- 240ml cream
- 240ml milk
- 250ml volume of dry brown bread crumbs (use a dense, dark brown bread that is quite stale)
- 15ml (1 tablespoon) water
- 80g dark brown sugar

A tip from our kitchen:

If you don't have stale bread, you could use a fresh loaf in a pinch. Break it into crumbs, spread it on a baking tray, and bake it at low temperature (50C) for a couple of hours to dry it out.

Recipe continues ...

Seán's Favourite
Pairing:

You can make
a dramatic and
delicious dessert
by floating a scoop
of brown bread ice
cream in a 'bath'
of Irish stout.

(you should have soft peaks – don't over-whip).

13. Fold the cream (gently stir) into the custard.

14. Freeze using a domestic ice cream machine, or cover and place in the freezer, stirring every few hours to break up the ice crystals.

15. Add the bread crumbs when the ice cream has become reasonably solid.

16. If you're using a domestic ice cream machine, transfer to a freezer-proof covered container when the ice cream has achieved a semi-solid consistency (around 15 minutes). Place it in the freezer, and continue to freeze until it is solid.

Yield: 8 servings

Notes:

o   Make sure the bread is stale or dry, or it will be very chewy in the ice cream.

o   To pasteurise the eggs, heat the custard to 73C and maintain that temperature for at least 5 minutes. Use a cooking thermometer, though, and keep stirring! If the custard goes any higher than 76C, the eggs will scramble. Immediately cover and place in the freezer until cool.

CHOCOLATE WHISKEY (FUISCE) ICE CREAM

There seems to be some disagreement as to whether the Irish or the Scots invented whiskey, although the first written account (in 1405) is Irish – a monk happily distilling away. It's very likely that whiskey pre-dates this record, and there are even some who say that none other than St. Patrick brought the method of distilling when he arrived on this island. We're happy to claim it, and there are few better uses than with chocolate. The earthy flavour and alcoholic tang of a strong whiskey add a great deal to chocolate, whether

it be in truffles, in a sauce or in ice cream. We call this flavour 'Fuisce,' and it is one of our top-sellers.

I can't say the idea of pairing chocolate and whiskey was ours. Seán went through a stage of being quite addicted to chocolate whiskey truffles made here in Ireland. He wanted to wean himself and making an ice cream equivalent seemed a good idea. It proved far more successful than we had dreamed, with customers loving the smoothness and character of the flavour. This is Seán's favourite flavour – so much so that he has even given up the truffles. The only question, as we played around with formulation, was which whiskey we should use, so we tried the full gamut. Lighter whiskeys get lost under the weight of dark chocolate, so we decided it's best to use something with a full flavour and a lot of bite. Such a whiskey might not be to your taste when it comes to tippling away, but it works best in ice cream.

WHAT TO DO:

1. Melt the chocolate in a double boiler over simmering water or in a microwave. Take care – chocolate melts at a low temperature (approx. 37C) and it burns easily, so once it's melted, remove from the heat!

2. Beat the sugar and egg yolks together until pale yellow.

3. Bring the milk to a low simmer.

4. Remove from the heat and beat the milk into the egg and sugar mixture in a slow stream. Pour the mixture back into the pan and place over low heat.

5. Stir continuously until the custard thickens slightly (around 65–70C) and just coats the back of a spoon. Don't over-heat, though, because at around 76C you will scramble the eggs! Immediately remove from the heat.

6. Add to the melted chocolate in small parts and mix thoroughly until smooth and velvety.

Ingredients:

- 100g sugar
- 4 egg yolks
- 220ml milk
- 200ml cream
- 150g dark (70%) chocolate
- 45ml (3 tablespoons) whiskey

7. Cover the chocolate custard with plastic wrap and refrigerate until cool.

8. Stir in the whiskey.

9. Whip the cream until it has doubled in volume (you should have soft peaks – don't over-whip).

10. Fold the cream (gently stir) into the custard.

11. Freeze using a domestic ice cream machine, or cover and place in the freezer, stirring every few hours to break up the ice crystals.

12. If you're using a domestic ice cream machine, transfer to a freezer-proof covered container when the ice cream has achieved a semi-solid consistency (around 15 minutes). Place it in the freezer, and continue to freeze until it is solid.

Yield: 8 servings.

Notes:

o   The chocolate and the custard must both be warm when you mix them, or you won't get a good emulsion. It's also important to add the custard to the chocolate in small parts, incorporating it each time by stirring.

o   To pasteurise the eggs, heat the custard to 73C and maintain that temperature for at least 5 minutes. Use a cooking thermometer, and keep stirring! If the custard goes any higher than 76C, the eggs will scramble. Immediately cover and place in the freezer until cool.

GRÁ SEACLÁID (CHOCOLATE LOVE) ICE CREAM

In the very early days of Murphys Ice Cream, Seán and I concentrated mostly on re-creating flavours that we knew and loved. Filling an ice cream cabinet is hard work, if you want to make each ice cream special, and it took us quite a while until we had the classics sorted to our (and our customers') satisfaction. Once we had them, we talked about what flavours we wanted to add, and, being chocaholics, the first had to be a chocolate flavour. We wanted something a little more complex, a little richer, with a stronger bite of chocolate. 'Grá Seacláid' became our very first invention, created through endless trials in our Dingle kitchen. From the moment we brought it out, people loved it, and it is still as popular today.

Chocolate and raspberry has always been one my favourite combinations, and raspberries one of my favourite fruits. We had raspberries growing in our garden when I grew up, and I spent hours plucking the plump red berries and popping them in my mouth. For me, there is no berry as velvety, delicious and deeply satisfying. With all the gorging in the garden, I never became sick of them. As for the chocolate, we wanted to have a stronger taste of bittersweet chocolate and experimented with chocolate chips. They had a satisfying crunch, but we started using chocolate shavings because they melt so quickly on the palate, releasing a chocolate hit almost instantaneously.

We hope this is an ice cream to really make you and your loved ones feel special. Make it with love, and you will see why the name contains that word within it – when it comes to using your spoons.

Ingredients:

- 100g + 20g sugar
- 4 egg yolks
- 220ml milk
- 200ml cream
- 150g + 20g dark (70%) chocolate
- 125g fresh raspberries

You may not know:

Besides North America, raspberries are also indigenous to Turkey and was a great favourite of the people of ancient Troy (Troas).

WHAT TO DO:

1. Put the raspberries in a pan and cook with the 20g of the sugar over low heat, stirring constantly until sugar is completely dissolved.

2. Press the hot raspberries through a sieve with a spoon or spatula to remove the seeds, then allow to cool completely.

3. Melt 150g chocolate in a double boiler over simmering water or in a microwave. Take care – chocolate melts at a low temperature (approx. 37C) and it burns easily!

4. Beat the rest of sugar and egg yolks together until pale yellow.

5. Bring the milk to a low simmer.

6. Remove from the heat and beat the milk into the egg and sugar mixture in a slow stream. Pour the mixture back into the pan and place over low heat.

7. Stir continuously until the custard thickens slightly (around 65–70C) and just coats the back of a spoon. Don't over-heat, though, because at around 76C you will scramble the eggs! Immediately remove from the heat.

8. Add to the melted chocolate in small parts and mix thoroughly until smooth and velvety.

9. Cover the chocolate custard with plastic wrap and refrigerate until cool.

10. Stir in the pureed raspberries.

11. Whip the cream until it has doubled in volume (you should have soft peaks – don't over-whip).

12. Fold the cream (gently stir) into the custard.

13. Use a potato peeler or cheese grater to create chocolate shavings with the remaining 20g of chocolate, and stir into the mix.

14. Freeze using a domestic ice cream machine, or cover and place in the freezer, stirring every few hours to break up the ice crystals.

15. If you're using a domestic ice cream machine, transfer to a freezer-proof covered container when the ice cream has achieved a semi-solid consistency (around 15 minutes). Place it in the freezer, and continue to freeze until it is solid.

Yield: 8 servings

Notes:

o   The chocolate and the custard must both be warm when you mix them, or you won't get a good emulsion. It's also important to add the custard to the chocolate in small parts, incorporating it each time by stirring.

o   To pasteurise the eggs, heat the custard to 73C and maintain that temperature for at least 5 minutes. Use a cooking thermometer, though! If the custard goes any higher than 76C, the eggs will scramble. Immediately cover and place in the freezer until cool.

A tip from our kitchen:

You could always double the amount of raspberries, cook as described above, and use the second half as a topping for the ice cream.

Seán's Favourite Pairing:

Make a chocolate sundae with this flavour, using hot fudge sauce and a topping of fresh raspberries.

'Stout', when referring to ale, simply means strong. The original term would have been 'stout porter,' referring to a strong, dark ale, but the porter part has gotten lost along the way.

Ingredients:

- 130g sugar
- 5 egg yolks
- 240ml cream
- 200ml milk
- 500ml Guinness
- A handful of dark chocolate chips

GUINNESS (PÓRTAR) ICE CREAM

More and more Irish might be choosing a bottle of wine at home instead of a night at the pub, but I like going out on a Saturday night. In a small town like Dingle, chances are you'll meet people you haven't seen for a while, learn something you've never known, and leave happy with the warmth of porter in your belly.

When we first decided to try making a Guinness ice cream, I ordered a couple of pints next door, left, and returned a few minutes later with a container big enough to fit both. The head had settled nicely as the black pints sat on the counter, and a few afternoon drinkers nodded at me, perhaps surprised to see me in at that hour. I paid the bartender and then poured the pints into the container. The atmosphere in the pub turned positively frosty. The drinkers stared in shocked silence, and the bartender exclaimed, 'How could you do that to two perfect pints?' I don't think I braved that particular pub again for a couple of months.

The ice cream, however, turned out a treat. I might suggest that if you make this flavour, you don't repeat my mistake. Purchase cans of Guinness that you can pour out in the privacy of your own home. Otherwise, you might lose your favourite public house!

WHAT TO DO:

1. Measure out 100ml of Guinness and set aside.
2. Boil the remaining 400ml Guinness until it reduces to 100ml in volume. Cool.
3. Beat the sugar and egg yolks together until thick and pale yellow.
4. Bring the milk to a low simmer.
5. Slowly beat the milk into the eggs and sugar.
6. Pour the mixture back into the pan and place over low heat.

7. Stir continuously until the custard thickens slightly (around 65–70C) and just coats the back of a spoon. Don't over-heat, though, because at around 76C you will scramble the eggs!

8. Immediately remove from the heat.

9. Transfer the custard into a small container, cover, and refrigerate until cool (5C).

10. Stir in both the reduced and non-reduced Guinness.

11. Whip the cream until it has doubled in volume (you should have soft peaks – don't over-whip).

12. Fold the cream (gently stir) into the custard.

13. Freeze using a domestic ice cream machine, or cover and place in the freezer, stirring every few hours to break up the ice crystals.

14. Add the chocolate chips when the ice cream has become semi-solid, or they will all sink to the bottom.

15. If you're using a domestic ice cream machine, transfer to a freezer-proof covered container when the ice cream has achieved a semi-solid consistency (around 15 minutes). Place it in the freezer, and continue to freeze until it is solid.

Yield: 8 servings

Notes:

o   You don't have to use the chocolate chips of course, but I do think Guinness and chocolate go well together.

o   To pasteurise the eggs, heat the custard to 73C and maintain that temperature for at least 5 minutes. Use a cooking thermometer, though! If the custard goes any higher than 76C, the eggs will scramble. Immediately cover and place in the freezer until cool.

A tip from our kitchen:

We combine reduced and non-reduced Guinness because using just reduced loses a bit of freshness and using non-reduced turns the ice cream icy.

Seán's Favourite Pairing:

You can make Guinness ice cream truffles by pouring the ice cream, just out of the machine, into a baking dish. Freeze solid, and when it's hard, cut it into squares. Pour over melted chocolate and return to the freezer. Now you have a really unique dessert!

IRISH COFFEE (CAIFE GAELACH) ICE CREAM

Between 1939 and 1945, the centre for Irish aviation was at a place on the Shannon called Foynes. It catered to the very first non-stop commercial flight from the US to Europe, and it became the hub for European aviation for a brief period. The planes were called 'flying boats,' since they landed in the water, and it was only later that airplanes landed on the ground and the airport moved to its present location at Shannon. In the meantime, American soldiers going off to war, businessmen, politicians, and movie stars used the airport at Foynes. The flights took a staggering 25 hours, and even though the planes were considered luxurious, passengers would have been dazed, tired, and shaken when they landed.

There was a café and restaurant in the terminal, quite important, as passengers had to wait while the plane was prepared for the next leg of the journey. The chef, a Tyrone man named Joe Sheridan, quickly realised that his customers needed something a bit stronger in their coffee. The wait in the airport could be long, the weather cold and rainy, and he took to adding a bit of whiskey to the steaming brew. The drink became famous, spread world-wide and I'm sure has since warmed the hearts of many thousands of both passengers and those hardly inclined to travel.

In ice cream, coffee and whiskey make for a smooth combination. It might be the perfect one to eat on a rainy day while dreaming of travel to exotic, faraway places in the sun.

You may not know:

Many famous people passed through Foynes, including Charles Lindbergh, John F Kennedy, Humphrey Bogart, Ernest Hemingway, and Eleanor Roosevelt, who travelled under the hardly original pseudonym of 'Mrs. Smith.'

Ingredients:

- 150g sugar
- 5 egg yolks
- 240ml cream
- 200ml milk
- 200ml espresso
- 45ml (3 tablespoons) Irish whiskey

WHAT TO DO:

1. Add 50g of the sugar to the espresso and reduce over medium heat until it is about one-third of its volume. Cool.

2. Beat in the egg yolks with the rest of the sugar until thick and pale yellow.

3. Bring the milk to a low simmer.

4. Beat the milk into the eggs and sugar in a slow stream.

5. Pour the mixture back into the pan and place over low heat.

6. Stir continuously until the custard thickens slightly (around 65–70C) and just coats the back of a spoon. Don't over-heat, though, because at around 76C you will scramble the eggs!

7. Immediately remove from the heat.

8. Transfer the custard into a small container, cover, and refrigerate until cool (5C).

9. Stir in the espresso and the whiskey.

10. Whip the cream until it has doubled in volume (you should have soft peaks – don't over-whip).

11. Fold the cream (gently stir) into the custard.

12. Freeze using a domestic ice cream machine, or cover and place in the freezer, stirring every few hours to break up the ice crystals.

13. If you're using a domestic ice cream machine, transfer to a freezer-proof covered container when the ice cream has achieved a semi-solid consistency (around 15 minutes). Place it in the freezer, and continue to freeze until it is solid.

Yield: 8 servings

Note:

o To pasteurise the eggs, heat the custard to 73C and maintain that temperature for at least 5 minutes. Use a cooking thermometer, though! If the custard goes any higher than 76C, the eggs will scramble. Immediately cover and place in the freezer until cool.

A tip from our kitchen:

You can make an amazing coffee concentrate that you can use for baking or as a sauce by reducing espresso and sugar until it's dark and caramelised.

Seán's Favourite Pairing:

Make an ice cream Irish coffee. Put a scoop of Irish Coffee ice cream in a coffee cup, add hot coffee and top with cream. Extra whiskey optional!

Book of Sweet Things

IRISH CREAM LIQUEUR (BÓ BHÁN) ICE CREAM

In 1974, the world's first Irish cream liqueur hit the shelves, and within a few short decades it became so popular that there is scarcely a pub in the world where you couldn't order one. On a trip to Argentina, out in the wilds of cowboy country, I spotted it on the shelves of a ramshackle bar that had a choice of only fifteen bottles of booze. It's an amazing Irish success story, and one that deserves to be celebrated, whether or not it's your choice of a tipple. With cream, alcohol, whiskey, and hints of coffee and chocolate, it's everything naughty rolled into one. Well, everything except ice cream, and making it into an ice cream amplifies the indulgence. We've made this flavour since our early days, and we called it, 'bó bhán,' meaning 'white cow.'

It's a great favourite in our shops and among the restaurateurs we supply. Chefs like it because it goes very well with many desserts, and our customers like because it is Irish and has so many pleasant associations. Mind you, most adults like this ice cream once they taste it because it is so creamy and delicious. The alcohol gives it a soft and smooth consistency and a nice little bite. Make it for a dinner party either on its own or with another dessert, and it will disappear very quickly indeed.

You may not know:

Traditionally, even the alcohol in Irish cream liqueurs came from the cow – distilled from dairy left-overs.

A tip from our kitchen:

If you want the taste of the Irish cream liqueur without the alcohol, you can always add it before you cook the custard, and most (if not all) should evaporate.

WHAT TO DO:

1. Beat the sugar and egg yolks together until thick and pale yellow.

2. Bring the milk to a low simmer. Remove from the heat.

3. Beat the milk into the eggs and sugar in a slow stream.

4. Pour the mixture back into the pan and place over low heat.

5. Stir continuously until the custard thickens slightly (around 65–70C) and just coats the back of a spoon. Don't over-heat, though, because at around 76C you will scramble the eggs!

6. Immediately remove from the heat.

7. Transfer the custard into a small container, cover, and refrigerate until cool (5C).

8. Mix in the cream and the liqueur, beating for one minute.

9. Freeze using a domestic ice cream machine, or cover and place in the freezer, stirring every few hours to break up the ice crystals.

10. If you're using a domestic ice cream machine, transfer to a freezer-proof covered container when the ice cream has achieved a semi-solid consistency (around 15 minutes). Place it in the freezer, and continue to freeze until it is solid.

Yield: 8 servings

Ingredients:

- 130g sugar
- 5 egg yolks
- 240ml cream
- 200 ml milk
- 45ml (3 table-spoons) Irish Cream Liqueur (we suggest Baileys, and you can add a bit more if you want, but if you add too much, the ice cream will be very soft and melt quickly)

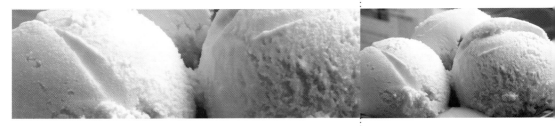

Notes:

o   Make sure you add the liqueur when the mixture is cool, or the alcohol will evaporate.

o   I haven't whipped the cream for this flavour, since I like it dense and rich. However, if you want a lighter ice cream, whip the cream before adding it to the custard.

o   To pasteurise the eggs, heat the custard to 73C and maintain that temperature for at least 5 minutes. Use a cooking thermometer, though, and keep stirring! If the custard goes any higher than 76C, the eggs will scramble. Immediately cover and place in the freezer until cool.

Seán's Favourite Pairing:

Customers in our Killarney shop have suggested (and devour) the following – a warm brownie with Irish Cream Liqueur Ice Cream and a good measure of heated chocolate sauce. I tend to agree. It's a brilliant combination.

LEMON CURD (LÍOMÓID) ICE CREAM

We recently had a restaurant that wanted a lemon ice cream, and J.P., our production manager, suggested that we try something a little less traditional and formulate a lemon curd ice cream. Lemon curd? I can't say the idea would have been foremost in my mind. Still, knowing full well that you should never judge an ice cream until you taste it and that J.P. should not be underestimated, I told him to go ahead and see what he could do. Not only did he add the requisite preserves to his new flavour, he included a healthy dose of lemon zest (grated peel). The restaurateur was delighted with J.P.'s creation, and the customers in the shops gave it glowing reviews as well. For me, the more I tasted it, the more I liked it. J.P. had done extremely well.

I think what makes this ice cream so good is that combination of zest and preserves. I love any kind of citrus zest in cooking – it's brilliant and fresh and can lift almost anything. The preserves add a richness and fullness that can't be found with just lemon juice and zest. If you didn't know what you were tasting, you would recognise lemon straightaway, but there might be some difficulty in placing the earthy undertones that makes this ice cream so distinctive. It's far more complex than any lemon ice cream I have ever come across, and it's become a regular in our scooping cabinet. Although lemon curd itself is a British invention, J.P.'s expert formulation has made this an Irish flavour.

You may not know:

Lemons probably originated in India, although they came to prominence in the Islamic world, where they were prized for their fruit and used in decorative gardens.

WHAT TO DO:

1. Beat in the egg yolks with the rest of the sugar until thick and pale yellow.
2. Bring the milk to a low simmer.
3. Beat the milk into the eggs and sugar in a slow stream.

4. Pour the mixture back into the pan and place over low heat.

5. Stir continuously until the custard thickens slightly (around 65–70C) and just coats the back of a spoon. Don't over-heat, though, because at around 76C you will scramble the eggs!

6. Immediately remove from the heat.

7. Add the lemon curd to the warm custard, stirring until it is dissolved.

8. Add the lemon zest.

9. Cover the custard with plastic wrap and refrigerate until cool overnight.

10. Strain the lemon zest from the cool custard (unless you like it in there).

11. Whip the cream until it has doubled in volume (you should have soft peaks – don't over-whip).

12. Fold the cream (gently stir) into the custard.

13. Add the lemon juice.

14. Freeze using a domestic ice cream machine, or cover and place in the freezer, stirring every few hours to break up the ice crystals.

15. If you're using a domestic ice cream machine, transfer to a freezer-proof covered container when the ice cream has achieved a semi-solid consistency (around 15 minutes). Place it in the freezer, and continue to freeze until it is solid.

Yield: 8 servings

Note:

o   To pasteurise the eggs, heat the custard to 73C and maintain that temperature for at least 5 minutes. Use a cooking thermometer, though! If the custard goes any higher than 76C, the eggs will scramble. Immediately cover and place in the freezer until cool.

Ingredients:

- 130g sugar
- 5 egg yolks
- 240ml cream
- 200ml milk
- 50g lemon curd
- Zest (grated peel) of one lemon
- 15ml (1 tablespoon) lemon juice

A tip from our kitchen:

Make sure you add the lemon curd while the custard is warm, or you might have some trouble getting it to dissolve fully.

Seán's Favourite Pairing:

Lemon and ginger is a great combination and so is lemon and meringue. Try Lemon Curd Ice Cream on a soft meringue and top with crumbled ginger biscuits.

SHERRY TRIFLE (TRAIDHFIL) ICE CREAM

For many Irish people of my father's age, there is hardly a dessert that compares to trifle. In fact, it's my father's favourite dessert. Finbarr grew up with it in Cork, where his family enjoyed it on special occasions. He likes his trifle booze-free, and that is how my Aunt Carol made it for us as children, with delicious fruit and dollops of fresh cream. She made it in a big casserole dish, but somehow there never seemed to be any left over for the next day. We ate trifle often, especially around Christmas, and it still brings back fond memories. None of us really cared for heavy Christmas cakes or puddings. Trifle is rare among yuletide treats in that it need not be overly heavy. A good trifle can end a meal on a high note, with no lingering after-effects.

Trifle is another dessert that came to us from across the Irish Sea, and it used to be even lighter. In Elizabethan times, it was simply cream, rose water, ginger, and sugar whipped into a froth. A translator referred to it in 1598 as 'a kinde of clouted creame called a foole or a trifle in English." Not until the eighteenth century were biscuits or macaroons added, and trifle took on the form we know today. Mind you, there is always a lot of argument about the proper way to make trifle. Is there jelly (gelatine)? Fresh fruit or canned fruit? Sponge or ladyfingers? What's the booze? Sweet or dry sherry? I've allowed latitude in the recipe (feel free to substitute the alcohol). I'm not a fan of jelly in anything and certainly not in ice cream, so that goes, and please don't mention custard from a box! I like the kick of brandy, so there is a fair bit of it.

This is really a Christmas flavour, and it might just be the perfect thing for those evenings after the big meal, when you still have family or guests around but have run out of dessert ideas. You can make this ahead of time and keep it in the freezer until something special is needed to perk up your loved ones.

You may not know:

There's no known origin of the word 'trifle,' as it relates to the dessert, but I love the normal connotations of the word, such as 'almost nothing,' 'light,' and 'frivolous.'

WHAT TO DO:

1. (Day before) Cut the fruit in small pieces, combine with the brandy, cover, and soak over night. If you use fruit cocktail from a can, drain off all the liquid first. This part is important, or the fruit will become very icy in the ice cream. The absorbed alcohol will minimise the iciness.

2. Combine the sponge or ladyfingers with the sherry. Stir until it is absorbed.

3. Beat the sugar and egg yolks together until thick and pale yellow.

4. Bring the milk to a low simmer. Remove from the heat.

5. Beat the milk into the eggs and sugar in a slow stream.

6. Pour the mixture back into the pan and place over low heat.

7. Stir continuously until the custard thickens slightly (around 65–70C) and just coats the back of a spoon. Don't over-heat, though, because at around 76C you will scramble the eggs!

8. Immediately remove from the heat.

9. Transfer the custard into a small container, cover, and refrigerate until cool (5C).

10. Whip the cream until you have soft peaks. Do not over-whip!

11. Fold the cream (gently stir) into the custard.

12. Stir in the sponge.

13. Freeze using a domestic ice cream machine, or cover and place in the freezer, stirring every few hours to break up the ice crystals.

14. Add the fruit when the ice cream has become semi-solid.

15. If you're using a domestic ice cream machine, transfer to a freezer-proof covered container when the ice cream has achieved a semi-solid consist-

Ingredients:

- 130g sugar
- 5 egg yolks
- 240ml cream
- 200ml milk
- 40ml brandy
- 40ml sherry
- 150ml volume crushed sponge or ladyfingers
- 150ml volume mixed fruit or fruit cocktail

A tip from our kitchen:

Almond biscuits or macaroons can make for an interesting substitution for the normal ladyfingers or sponge cake.

Recipe continues …

Book of Sweet Things

Continue the trifle
theme. Serve it
with fresh fruit
and cream.

ency (around 15 minutes). Place it in the freezer, and continue to freeze until it is solid.

Yield: 8 Servings

Notes:

o   Because of the alcohol in this recipe, it will melt more quickly than normal ice cream.

o   To pasteurise the eggs, heat the custard to 73C and maintain that temperature for at least 5 minutes. Use a cooking thermometer, though, and keep stirring! If the custard goes any higher than 76C, the eggs will scramble. Immediately cover and place in the freezer until cool.

STRAWBERRY AND SAGE (SÁISTE) ICE CREAM

Recently, we have been using some fresh herbs in our ice creams, and sage has always been one of my favourites. It makes Seán and me think of Texas, where we lived, of gardens and hot, sun-baked stucco walls with little lizards scurrying up them. Many towns in the southwestern US are redolent with purple sage, and the bushes grow rampantly. Of course, here in Ireland, we don't have much sun-baked anything, but I do have a modest little sage plant growing quite happily in my back yard. Sage complements fresh strawberries perfectly – together the flavours seem so inter-twined that it's almost hard to imagine separating them!

We're lucky in Ireland in that we have an abundance of wonderful, fresh strawberries in season. Wexford or Wicklow strawberries straight from the farm shame the pale imitation that clutter up our supermarket shelves most of the year. For me at least, they scream for inclusion in ice cream. There's a farm in Co. Wicklow called 'Sweetbank' that gives us fruit and sells our ice cream in their farm shop, and we're always delighted for it. We come back with crates that perfume our production facility for days.

For the following recipe, don't bother making it unless you have some red, ripe strawberries. I definitely suggest using fresh sage as well in this recipe, which you should be able to find in your supermarket if you don't have some in your garden. The whole idea here is to try to freeze a bit of summer, and you should have an ice cream with a wonderful pink colour and a bright, aromatic flavour.

The sage shouldn't over-power, and you don't even have to tell squeamish children of a certain age that it is there at all. Although we did have a little fellow in Killarney complain about the 'green bits,' most would never notice it.

WHAT TO DO:

1. Rinse and hull the strawberries.
2. Put them in a food processor or blender with the water and 2 teaspoons of the sugar and pulse two or three times. You don't want a puree here! Just break them up a bit.
3. Chop the sage leaves into fine pieces. (If you use dried sage, use about a half teaspoon).
4. Combine the blended strawberries and the sage in a sauce pan and cook over low heat for about 10 minutes. Don't bring it to the boil. Cook it slowly simply to infuse the strawberries with the sage.
5. Allow to cool.
6. Add the lemon.
7. In a separate bowl, beat the sugar and egg yolks together until thick and pale yellow.
8. Bring the milk to a low simmer. Remove from the heat.
9. Beat the milk into the eggs and sugar in a slow stream.
10. Pour the mixture back into the pan and place over

Ingredients:

- 130g + 2 teaspoons sugar
- 5 egg yolks
- 240ml cream
- 200ml milk
- 150g fresh strawberries
- 15ml (1 tablespoon) water
- 15ml (1 tablespoon) lemon
- 2 fresh sage leaves

Recipe continues …

Book of Sweet Things

You may not know:

Both strawberries and sage originated in the Mediterranean, and both were prized for their medicinal properties. In fact, 'Sage' comes from the Latin 'Salveo,' which means 'to heal.'

A tip from our kitchen:

You can always hold back a little of the cooked strawberry and sage puree (coulis) and use it later as a colourful decorative topping for the ice cream.

Seán's Favourite Pairing:

A nice touch is to serve this on a plate that has been drizzled with a little bit of balsamic vinegar. Garnish with fresh mint or basil.

low heat.

11. Stir continuously until the custard thickens slightly (around 65–70C) and just coats the back of a spoon. Don't over-heat, though, because at around 76C you will scramble the eggs!
12. Immediately remove from the heat.
13. Transfer the custard into a small container, cover, and refrigerate until cool (5C).
14. Whip the cream until it has doubled in volume (you should have soft peaks – don't over-whip).
15. Fold the cream (gently stir) into the custard.
16. Stir in the sage-infused strawberries.
17. Freeze using a domestic ice cream machine, or cover and place in the freezer, stirring every few hours to break up the ice crystals.
18. If you're using a domestic ice cream machine, transfer to a freezer-proof covered container when the ice cream has achieved a semi-solid consistency (around 15 minutes). Place it in the freezer, and continue to freeze until it is solid.

Yield: 8 servings

Note:

o To pasteurise the eggs, heat the custard to 73C and maintain that temperature for at least 5 minutes. Use a cooking thermometer, though, and keep stirring! If the custard goes any higher than 76C, the eggs will scramble. Immediately cover and place in the freezer until cool.

Ice Cream Recipes with International Flair

The world is getting smaller as we travel abroad more often and as others visit us in Ireland, allowing a sharing of cultures and culinary ideas.

These recipes are some of my favourite tastes from around the world. Whether found on a trip or passed on by customers in our shops, the following flavours have become a part of Murphys Ice Cream.

BAKALIOWE ICE CREAM

Since I've moved here, Ireland has changed dramatically. My father's whole family had to emigrate abroad for work opportunities, but now he's returned, joining hundreds and thousands of both Irish and non-Irish seeking a better life in Ireland. The range of immigrants is remarkable – every continent is represented among our population, and the list of countries is a long one. There are those who bemoan the changed Ireland, but I find it fascinating. It's an opportunity to learn new things and expand horizons. For example, I knew nothing about the tiny South Pacific Island of New Caledonia until we hired Christophe, who hails from there and works as part of our production team.

In any given season, we could employ Irish, Poles, Czechs, English, Russians, French, Italians, Spanish and other nationalities, and I think both our team and our customers are enriched by the variety. It certainly helps that the people we hire share our love for ice cream, coffees and chocolate. No matter how different our traditions, and whether we call it 'ice cream,' 'lody,' 'zmrzlina,' or 'glace,' we all find it tasty on a sunny (or rainy) day!

I always ask a new team member from another country about their ice cream speciality, and we have benefited from many ideas and recipes. According to Sylwia, who worked in our Killarney shop, the following ice cream is the best-selling Polish flavour. It's so interesting that I thought I'd have to include it in the book, and I thank Sylwia and our other Polish staff for helping me get it right.

WHAT TO DO:

1. Beat the sugar and egg yolks together until thick and pale yellow.

2. Bring the milk to a low simmer. Remove from the heat.

3. Beat the milk into the eggs and sugar in a slow stream.

4. Pour the mixture back into the pan, add the vanilla bean and place over low heat.

5. Stir continuously until the custard thickens slightly (around 65–70C) and just coats the back of a spoon. Don't over-heat, though, because at around 76C you will scramble the eggs!

6. Immediately remove from the heat.

7. Transfer the custard into a small container, cover, and refrigerate until cool (5C).

8. Remove the vanilla bean.

9. Whip the cream until it has doubled in volume (you should have soft peaks – don't over-whip).

10. Fold the cream (gently stir) into the custard.

11. Freeze using a domestic ice cream machine, or cover and place in the freezer, adding the dried nuts and fruit when it has already become semi-solid.

12. If you're using a domestic ice cream machine, transfer to a freezer-proof covered container when the ice cream has achieved a semi-solid consistency (around 15 minutes). Place it in the freezer, and continue to freeze until it is solid.

8 servings

Note:

o To pasteurise the eggs, heat the custard to 73C and maintain that temperature for at least 5 minutes. Use a cooking thermometer, though, and keep stirring! If the custard goes any higher than 76C, the eggs will scramble. Immediately cover and place in the freezer until cool.

Ingredients:

- 130g sugar
- 5 egg yolks
- 240ml cream
- 200ml milk
- ¼ vanilla bean, cut lengthwise
- 60g raisins
- 50g other dried fruits (chopped)
- 40g almonds and other nuts

Seán's Favourite Pairing:

Our Polish staff tells us that the only way to eat this ice cream is on a cone. We defer to their judgment.

CARDAMOM HONEY (MIL) ICE CREAM

Two years ago, I visited Morocco – a holiday bought on a whim in the search for Winter sun. I liked the country far better that I ever thought I would. In fact, the richness of culture and cuisine won me over completely. From the mountain town of Tafraoute, with its dramatic pink rock formations, to the quiet splendour of the Sahara, to the splendid walled, sea-side port of Essaouira, the country beguiled the eye and delighted the palate. In between visiting teeming markets or breathtaking landscapes, one could dine on fresh breads cooked in clay ovens, sizzling tagines of spiced vegetables, grilled fresh fish, and lovely pastries that embodied the sweet taste of a remarkable country.

Most Moroccan desserts use a combination of the following flavours – almond, honey, cardamom and rose. The honey and cardamom left the most indelible impressions. I love cardamom and was very happy that it made an appearance in dishes both sweet and savoury, and I'll never forget the honey. The best was made from the blossoms of the argan tree, and we bought jars of it on the roadside. With strong hints of caramel and amber colour, it was the best I have ever tasted. Had I driven over, I would have filled the car's boot with enough jars to last a couple of years.

This ice cream celebrates Morocco. For those of you who have been there, it might bring back some great memories. For those of you who haven't, I hope it will be an impetus to seek out that jewel of the desert.

WHAT TO DO:

1. Beat the sugar and egg yolks together until thick and pale yellow.

2. Bring the milk to a low simmer.

3. Beat the milk into the eggs and sugar in a slow stream.

You may not know:

One of the oddest sights in Morocco is the goats that climb the argan trees to eat the fruit. Perched up in the branches, they feast happily and undisturbed.

4. Pour the mixture back into the pan and place over low heat.

5. Stir continuously until the custard thickens slightly (around 65–70C) and just coats the back of a spoon. Don't over-heat, though, because at around 76C you will scramble the eggs!

6. Immediately remove from the heat.

7. Stir in the honey and cardamom.

8. Refrigerate overnight to infuse the mix with cardamom.

9. Pass the mix through a fine sieve to remove the cardamom bits.

10. Whip the cream until it has doubled in volume (you should have soft peaks – don't over-whip).

11. Fold the cream (gently stir) into the custard.

12. Freeze using a domestic ice cream machine, or cover and place in the freezer, stirring every few hours to break up the ice crystals.

13. If you're using a domestic ice cream machine, transfer to a freezer-proof covered container when the ice cream has achieved a semi-solid consistency (around 15 minutes). Place it in the freezer, and continue to freeze until it is solid.

Yield: 8 servings

Note:

o Spices can vary dramatically in potency, so vary the recipe if you find the cardamom to strong or not strong enough.

o To pasteurise the eggs, heat the custard to 73C and maintain that temperature for at least 5 minutes. Use a cooking thermometer, though, and keep stirring! If the custard goes any higher than 76C, the eggs will scramble. Immediately cover and place in the freezer until cool.

Ingredients:

- 130g sugar
- 5 egg yolks
- 240ml cream
- 200ml milk
- 5g (1 tablespoon) ground cardamom
- 65g (3 tablespoons) honey

A tip from our kitchen:

You don't always need to cook a spice to get its full flavour. Cold extractions can often give a fresher and brighter taste.

Seán's Favourite Pairing:

A scoop of Cardamom and a scoop of Pistachio ice cream together in a bowl need nothing else.

CIAN'S COFFEE BEAN CRUNCH ICE CREAM

This is a recipe we first made in the middle of August. It's our busiest time, a happy blur of activity. When I pull on my white coat and enter the lab I'm sure I must be one of the luckiest people alive. The smell of fresh cream and cooking chocolate, the crackle of toasting coconut and honeycomb pieces being broken into manageable chunks, the hum of the pasteuriser, the mixing and cooking, the tasting and tweaking of flavours – these are the things I love.

One day, Cian, our summer Dingle shop manager, suggested we make ice cream with chocolate-enrobed bits of coffee beans. I jumped at the idea. When in France or the States, in Barcelona, Venice, or anywhere I can find them, I devour chocolate coffee beans. The combination of dark chocolate and coffee has always been a big favourite, and the coffee beans also have such a satisfying crunch! Seán and I could share a whole bag at a single sitting.

Generally, we keep new flavours to a minimum in August, but we couldn't help ourselves. J.P., our production manager, cleared a couple hours on the schedule, and we all pitched in. Christophe melted chocolate, Cian crushed the coffee beans, J.P. prepared the ice cream, and we started playing around with the best combinations of taste and texture until we were happy. What fun! Here's the result, if you want to try it.

WHAT TO DO:

1. Melt the chocolate in a double boiler.
2. Break the coffee beans into smallish pieces using the bottom of a bowl or a food processor.
3. Mix the crushed beans into the chocolate and spread on a baking tray to harden.
4. Beat the sugar and egg yolks together until thick and pale yellow.

You may not know:

Coffee beans are not actually beans at all. They are the seed of a fruit, and not a vegetable! The confusion may have arisen from a bad translation of the original Arabic – 'qahwa' is coffee, and 'bunn' is berry.

5. Bring the milk to a low simmer. Remove from the heat.

6. Beat the milk into the eggs and sugar in a slow stream.

7. Pour the mixture back into the pan, add the vanilla bean and place over low heat.

8. Stir continuously until the custard thickens slightly (around 65–70C) and just coats the back of a spoon. Don't over-heat, though, because at around 76C you will scramble the eggs!

9. Immediately remove from the heat.

10. Remove the vanilla bean.

11. Transfer to another container, cover, and place in the refrigerator until cool (5C).

12. Cut the hardened chocolate into small pieces then use a spatula to separate from the baking tray.

13. Whip the cream until it has doubled in volume (you should have soft peaks – don't over-whip).

14. Fold the cream (gently stir) into the custard.

15. Freeze using a domestic ice cream machine, or cover and place in the freezer, adding the chocolate espresso beans when it's become semi-solid.

16. If you're using a domestic ice cream machine, transfer to a freezer-proof covered container when the ice cream has achieved a semi-solid consistency (around 15 minutes). Place it in the freezer, and continue to freeze until it is solid.

Yield: 8 servings

Note:

o   To pasteurise the eggs, heat the custard to 73C and maintain that temperature for at least 5 minutes. Use a cooking thermometer, though, and keep stirring! If the custard goes any higher than 76C, the eggs will scramble. Immediately cover and place in the freezer until cool.

Ingredients:

- 130g sugar
- 5 egg yolks
- 240ml cream
- 200ml milk
- ¼ vanilla bean, cut lengthwise
- 40g espresso beans
- 100g top quality 70% chocolate

Two tips from our kitchen:

We found the best espresso beans to be 'Sumatra.' When it comes time to cut up the chunks, decide how big you like them. Some like huge bits in their ice cream, and some prefer small …

CINNAMON LATTE ICE CREAM

Living in the United States in the early 1990s, Seán and I witnessed the coffee explosion that came out of Seattle and spread with astonishing rapidity to the entire country. We experienced a similar coffee boom here in Ireland a decade later. In America, from hardly being able to find a decent cappuccino, we were suddenly confronted with a coffee house on almost every street corner. Words like 'crema' and 'ristretto' became common parlance, as budding coffee connoisseurs obsessed about drinks they wouldn't have dreamed of just a few years earlier. Of course, the drink of choice, especially for busy urban professionals was the latte, and we watched the drinks grow to monstrous sizes in a short period of time. To me, the huge takeaway cup was a statement: 'I'm so busy, I need a coffee THIS big just to get me through the morning!'

Mind you, I like a large latte as much as anybody. A cappuccino or espresso is a better drink when I'm in a mood to appreciate them, perhaps in the afternoon, but they disappear awfully quickly. You get a great deal of sipping pleasure from a latte. Another change in the mid 1990s, besides the sizes, was the proliferation of flavoured lattes. Vanilla lattes, caramel lattes, hazelnut lattes, cinnamon lattes – it was possible to have almost any latte you could imagine at your local coffee house. We have seen the same trends come into Ireland, and no doubt they are here to stay (at least for a while!).

Given our damp climate, I think a warming spice such as cinnamon makes the best latte and also a wonderful ice cream. It's not too heavy on the coffee – just a nice balance of tastes.

Ingredients:

- 130g sugar
- 5 egg yolks
- 240ml cream
- 200ml milk
- 125ml espresso
- 1 teaspoon ground cinnamon

WHAT TO DO:

1. Add one tablespoon of the sugar to the espresso and reduce over medium heat until it is about one-third of its volume. Allow to cool.

2. Mix the cinnamon with the rest of the sugar, then beat in the egg yolks until thick and pale yellow.

3. Bring the milk to a low simmer.

4. Beat the milk into the eggs and sugar in a slow stream.

5. Pour the mixture back into the pan and place over low heat.

6. Stir continuously until the custard thickens slightly (around 65–70C) and just coats the back of a spoon. Don't over-heat, though, because at around 76C you will scramble the eggs!

7. Immediately remove from the heat.

8. Transfer the custard into a small container, cover, and refrigerate until cool (5C).

9. Stir in the reduced espresso.

10. Whip the cream until it has doubled in volume (you should have soft peaks – don't over-whip).

11. Fold the cream (gently stir) into the custard.

12. Freeze using a domestic ice cream machine, or cover and place in the freezer, stirring every few hours to break up the ice crystals.

13. If you're using a domestic ice cream machine, transfer to a freezer-proof covered container when the ice cream has achieved a semi-solid consistency (around 15 minutes). Place it in the freezer, and continue to freeze until it is solid.

Yield: 8 servings

Note:

o   To pasteurise the eggs, heat the custard to 73C and maintain that temperature for at least 5 minutes. Use a cooking thermometer, though, and keep stirring! If the custard goes any higher than 76C, the eggs will scramble. Immediately cover and place in the freezer until cool.

You may not know:

Don't order a 'latte' in Italy. 'Latte' means simply 'milk,' and that is likely what you will get. The term is 'caffè latte.'

A tip from our kitchen:

You can also use a cinnamon stick as described in the cinnamon ice cream recipe.

COCONUT AND RUM (CNÓ CÓCÓ) ICE CREAM

We concocted this recipe at the request of a restaurant in Dublin that wanted a coconut ice cream. When thinking about coconuts, I am filled with happy recollections. As a teenager, I visited the Caribbean and sampled the joys of rum and coconut. As an adult, one of the most amazing welcomes I have ever received was in an eco-village in Palolem, which is in Goa, India. There, scarcely had I set down my bag, when a man was dispatched with a machete in his teeth to fetch a coconut. I watched in awe as he clambered up a towering tree with great speed and agility and returned with the fruit. He chopped off the top with a couple strikes of his knife, pushed in two straws, and handed it to me to drink. I polished it off on the porch of my cabin, watching the palms sway by the seashore.

Back to the rum, though, and it is a great addition to coconut in ice cream. It's hard to get a good coconut flavour. Coconuts have a great deal of fat, and since fat blocks flavour, you can run into diminishing returns by adding more and more coconut. A solution that we found was to add coconut-flavoured rum, which should be easy enough to find. Not only does it boost the flavour, but it should get you into a happy, relaxed, Caribbean mood. Put on some music – reggae, perhaps, or steel drums, pull out the ice cream and kick back. It might be the rainiest day of the year, but you will bring in a lot of sunshine with this delicious flavour.

You may not know:

A coconut palm needs an atmosphere of high humidity and regular rainfall in which to grow. Don't get your hopes up though. It also needs abundant sunshine.

WHAT TO DO:

1. Beat the sugar and egg yolks together until thick and pale yellow.
2. Bring the milk to a low simmer.
3. Beat the milk into the eggs and sugar in a slow stream.

4. Pour the mixture back into the pan and place over low heat. Add the coconut milk.

5. Stir continuously until the custard thickens slightly (around 65–70C) and just coats the back of a spoon. Don't over-heat, though, because at around 76C you will scramble the eggs!

6. Immediately remove from the heat.

7. Refrigerate over night.

8. Toast the desiccated coconut over medium heat in a dry saucepan, stirring all the time, until they turn a golden colour. Allow to cool.

9. Stir the toasted coconut, rum and lemon juice into the refrigerated custard.

10. Whip the cream until it has doubled in volume (you should have soft peaks – don't over-whip).

11. Fold the cream (gently stir) into the custard.

12. Freeze using a domestic ice cream machine, or cover and place in the freezer, stirring every few hours to break up the ice crystals.

13. If you're using a domestic ice cream machine, transfer to a freezer-proof covered container when the ice cream has achieved a semi-solid consistency (around 15 minutes). Place it in the freezer, and continue to freeze until it is solid.

Notes:

o   Coconut milk has all different strengths, so taste it and make sure you're happy with the flavour. You can always add a bit more, but remember there will be more coconut flavour coming from the desiccated coconut and rum.

o   To pasteurise the eggs, heat the custard to 73C and maintain that temperature for at least 5 minutes. Use a cooking thermometer, though, and keep stirring! If the custard goes any higher than 76C, the eggs will scramble. Immediately cover and place in the freezer until cool.

Ingredients

- 130g sugar
- 5 egg yolks
- 240ml cream
- 200ml milk
- 175ml coconut milk
- 175ml volume (85g) desiccated (dried and shredded) coconut
- 60ml (about 4 tablespoons) coconut rum
- 15ml (1 tablespoon) lemon juice

A tip from our kitchen:

You can also use fresh coconut, if you have one to hand. To get out the milk, pierce two of the three 'eyes' (the second hole will allow air in) and drain it.

EARL GREY (TAE) ICE CREAM

Certainly one of the flavours I remember most as a teenager visiting London was Earl Grey tea. The aromatic whiff of bergamot from a steaming cup made the miserable weather almost palatable. It's not overly spiced, just a perfect, refined balance of tastes. I liked it so much that once I went off to college, I quickly adopted the habit of making a cup in my dorm room. While others drank coffee to keep themselves from dozing at their studies, I drank tea. I've become much more of a coffee drinker now, but every now and then when I want to feel a bit intellectual, I'll bring out the Earl Grey and feel transported back to those days of text books, deep conversations, and intense loves.

A few years after I left school, I found myself living in Somerville, a suburb of Boston. In nearby Cambridge, there was a famous little ice cream shop we used to frequent. They were known for strange and wonderful flavours, and one day I found Earl Grey ice cream in their cabinet. I ordered it, but I didn't expect to like it half as well as I did. Now, as I play around with the ice cream and learn more about chemistry, I know that the tannins in tea cut sweetness. Earl Grey tea generally has a mix of different black teas, including Darjeeling and China tea, but it is the bergamot that really make it distinctive. If you want an adult ice cream that will surprise your guests, this is one to try.

You may not know:

There was, of course, an Earl – Charles Grey, the 2nd Earl Grey, prime minister of England in the 1830s, who was an advocate of Catholic emancipation and helped to pass the abolition of slavery throughout the British Empire. It's said he received a gift of the tea from a diplomat and had a local tea house replicate the flavour.

Ingredients:

- 130g + 2 table-spoons sugar
- 5 egg yolks
- 240ml cream
- 250ml milk
- 6 Earl Grey tea bags or the loose leaf equivalent

WHAT TO DO:

1. Beat the sugar and egg yolks together until thick and pale yellow.
2. Bring the milk to a simmer.
3. Add the tea and allow to sit for 10 minutes.
4. Bring back to a low simmer, stir, and remove the tea bags.
5. Slowly beat the milk into the eggs and sugar.

6. Pour the mixture back into the pan and place over low heat.

7. Stir continuously until the custard thickens slightly (around 65–70C) and just coats the back of a spoon. Don't over-heat, though, because at around 76C you will scramble the eggs!

8. Immediately remove from the heat.

9. Transfer the custard into a small container, cover, and refrigerate until cool (5C).

10. Whip the cream until it has doubled in volume (you should have soft peaks – don't over-whip).

11. Fold the cream (gently stir) into the custard.

12. Freeze using a domestic ice cream machine, or cover and place in the freezer, stirring every few hours to break up the ice crystals.

13. If you're using a domestic ice cream machine, transfer to a freezer-proof covered container when the ice cream has achieved a semi-solid consistency (around 15 minutes). Place it in the freezer, and continue to freeze until it is solid.

Note:

o   To pasteurise the eggs, heat the custard to 73C and maintain that temperature for at least 5 minutes. Use a cooking thermometer, though, and keep stirring! If the custard goes any higher than 76C, the eggs will scramble. Immediately cover and place in the freezer until cool

A tip from our kitchen:

This flavour is strong. Just know that the longer you leave the tea in the milk, the stronger the flavour will be, so remove it earlier if you want a lighter flavour. If you stir gently while the tea is in the milk, you will extract more flavour.

Seán's Favourite Pairing:

This ice cream is absolutely perfect with a chocolate cake. It might sound an odd pairing, but there is nothing I can think of that goes better, except perhaps, more chocolate.

GELATO ALLA CREMA

You may not know:

Although some Italians might use the word 'cream' to describe this ice cream to an English speaker, 'panna' is the Italian for cream. 'crema' means 'custard' in this context.

Italy, for most people, is the home of ice cream. There is a story of Emperor Nero dispatching runners to the Apennines to bring back snow to be flavoured and served at the royal table. There is a tradition of artisan ice cream that goes back for many years, and an abundance of markets that provide some of the most beautiful fruits and other ice cream essentials. Industrial ice cream and prefabricated ice cream frozen on the premises has displaced many of the 'gelatai' (ice cream makers) in recent years, but in Italy, you can still find some of the best ice creams anywhere. It takes work to seek them out, however, for almost every gelateria has a sign outside labelling it as 'artisan,' whether they make it from scratch or not.

One way to test the quality of the ice cream is to sample their 'Crema.' The most popular flavour in Italy, 'Crema' is a plain frozen custard, that will reveal the standard of the ice cream. The following recipe is my tribute to the wonderful Italian tradition of ice cream and their great ice cream houses. With Irish cream and milk being so good, you should be able to make a delicious Gelato alla Grema. So, if you're planning a dinner of pasta or risotto, you might just consider ending it with a 'dolce' using this recipe. Buon appetito!

Ingredients:

- 500ml milk
- 250ml cream
- 200g sugar
- 6 egg yolks

WHAT TO DO

1. Beat the sugar and egg yolks together until thick and pale yellow.
2. Bring the milk to a low simmer.
3. Remove from the heat.
4. Beat the milk into the eggs and sugar in a slow stream.
5. Pour the mixture back into the pan and place over low heat.

6. Stir continuously until the custard thickens slightly (around 65–70C) and just coats the back of a spoon. Don't over-heat, though, because at around 76C you will scramble the eggs!

7. Immediately remove from the heat.

8. Transfer into another container, cover, and place in the refrigerator until cool (5C).

9. Whip the cream until it has doubled in volume (you should have soft peaks – don't over-whip).

10. Fold the cream (gently stir) into the custard.

11. Freeze using a domestic ice cream machine, or cover and place in the freezer, stirring every few hours to break up the ice crystals.

1. If you're using a domestic ice cream machine, transfer to a freezer-proof covered container when the ice cream has achieved a semi-solid consistency (around 15 minutes). Place it in the freezer, and continue to freeze until it is solid.

Yield: 8 servings

Note:

o   To pasteurise the eggs, heat the custard to 73C and maintain that temperature for at least 5 minutes. Use a cooking thermometer, though, and keep stirring! If the custard goes any higher than 76C, the eggs will scramble. Immediately cover and place in the freezer until cool

A tip from our kitchen:

If you are a fan of goat's milk, you can substitute it for the cow's milk in this recipe. Just know, however, that it will completely take over the flavour.

Seán's Favourite Pairing:

Fernando at Novecento Restaurant in Dingle suggests warming a baby croissant, hollowing it out, adding a scoop of Crema, and then serving it with a hot chocolate. Yum!

Book of Sweet Things

GREEN TEA AND GINGER (SINSÉAR) ICE CREAM

You may not know:

Green tea is green because it is not fermented like black tea, a process that turns the tea leaves black.

Ingredients:

- 130g sugar
- 5 egg yolks
- 240ml cream
- 250ml milk
- 2 tablespoon green tea leaves (4 bags)
- 60g crystallised ginger
- 1 tablespoon honey

Growing up in New York, Asian food was part of the staple diet. Whether Japanese, Thai, Vietnamese, Chinese, or Korean, the standard was high and the variety amazing. Some of the best meals I have ever eaten were Asian cooking. Oddly enough, great restaurants were not always in the heart of the city, although usually that was indeed the case. We frequented a Japanese restaurant in a small town upstate, where the residents were mostly Irish and Italian firemen and policemen who commuted into Manhattan. This restaurant was in a strip mall, but the minute you stepped through the doors, you knew it was special. A goldfish pond ran the length of the place, with little bridges joining the tables. The lighting was beautiful, the presentation superb, and my dessert of choice was green tea ice cream.

I wouldn't have usually tried such an ice cream as a teenager, but the other dessert option was a sticky rice pudding that didn't appeal to me much. Here in Ireland, I have also come across green tea ice cream in some of the ever-proliferating Asian restaurants, so perhaps you have tried it as well. If so, just be aware that since we don't believe in food colouring, and don't use the matcha (green tea powder) that is usually used for ice cream, it will not be bright green and will have a slightly different taste. For this recipe, I like to add crystallised ginger, a real favourite of mine. I love the spicy sweetness and intriguing consistency of the ginger, and it stays soft in the ice cream.

WHAT TO DO:

1. Heat the milk to a low simmer over medium heat.
2. Add the tea bags and honey and maintain at a simmer over low heat for about 10 minutes.
3. Remove from the heat and remove the tea bags.

4. Beat the sugar and egg yolks together until thick and pale yellow.
5. Beat the milky tea into the eggs and sugar in a slow stream.
6. Pour the mixture back into the pan and place over low heat.
7. Stir continuously until the custard thickens slightly (around 65–70C) and just coats the back of a spoon. Don't over-heat, though, because at around 76C you will scramble the eggs!
8. Immediately remove from the heat.
9. Transfer the custard into a small container, cover, and refrigerate until cool (5C).
10. Chop the crystallised ginger into small pieces.
11. Whip the cream until it has doubled in volume (you should have soft peaks – don't over-whip).
12. Fold the cream (gently stir) into the custard.
13. Freeze using a domestic ice cream machine, or cover and place in the freezer, stirring every few hours to break up the ice crystals.
14. Add the ginger once the ice cream has become semi-solid.
15. If you're using a domestic ice cream machine, transfer to a freezer-proof covered container when the ice cream has achieved a semi-solid consistency (around 15 minutes). Place it in the freezer, and continue to freeze until it is solid.

Yield: 8 servings

Note:

o   To pasteurise the eggs, heat the custard to 73C and maintain that temperature for at least 5 minutes. Use a cooking thermometer, though, and keep stirring! If the custard goes any higher than 76C, the eggs will scramble. Immediately cover and place in the freezer until cool.

A tip from our kitchen:

This recipe calls for cooking the tea for a long time, which works well for ice cream. However, when making green tea for drinking, make sure you don't steep the leaves for more than 3 minutes, or it will turn bitter.

Seán's Favourite Pairing:

Green tea ice cream with macadamia nuts and slices of fresh, sweet papaya puts me in a California-Asian-fusion cuisine state of mind.

HONEY LAVENDER (LABHANDAR) CREAM

A couple of years ago, I travelled across the South of France with a friend, eating our way from town to town. It was May, the weather was perfect, and the cuisine was mostly very good. As we drove, we passed purple fields of lavender – a flower used since ancient times for its antiseptic and other healing attributes. Most people know about the relaxing properties of lavender – some might even put a drop on their pillow if they have trouble falling asleep at night. It is less well known that it can be used for culinary purposes as well, and some of the French chefs we visited used it in both sweet and savoury dishes. The taste that really stayed with me after the trip was a simple pot of honey infused with lavender that I bought at a food market in San Rémy.

Upon returning to Ireland, I couldn't wait to make a honey lavender ice cream, and it turned out just as I had hoped. We have been serving it ever since, and when we cook the lavender flowers in production, the smell is intoxicating. Delivery drivers seem to take that little bit longer when looking for a signature, and the entire team spends the day completely chilled out. The taste in the ice cream is even better – a floral bouquet with all the goodness of French sunshine combined with the sweet complexity of honey. Customers have been enjoying it for years now, including one who had no sense of smell and finally was able to have some experience of such an exquisite scent. The ice cream is not for everyone, but those who like it will probably love it. If you make it at home, chances are your kids (if you have any) won't touch it, so you can eat it all yourself!

WHAT TO DO:

1. Cook the lavender flowers in the water over low heat until the water has reduced to 1/10th of the volume.

You may not know:

In ancient times, Lavender was called 'spikenard'. '...there came a woman having an alabaster box of ointment of spikenard very precious; and she brake the box, and poured it on his head.' - Gospel

of Mark, 14:3

Ingredients:

- 130g sugar
- 5 egg yolks
- 240ml cream
- 200ml milk
- 2 tablespoons lavender flowers
- 500ml water
- 3 tablespoons liquid honey

2. Remove from the heat, strain and stir in the honey.

3. Beat the sugar and egg yolks together until thick and pale yellow.

4. Bring the milk to a low simmer.

5. Beat the milk into the eggs and sugar in a slow stream.

6. Pour the mixture back into the pan and place over low heat.

7. Stir continuously until the custard thickens slightly (around 65–70C) and just coats the back of a spoon. Don't over-heat, though, because at around 76C you will scramble the eggs!

8. Immediately remove from the heat.

9. Transfer the custard into a small container, cover, and refrigerate until cool (5C).

10. Mix in the lavender and honey.

11. Whip the cream until it has doubled in volume (you should have soft peaks – don't over-whip).

12. Fold the cream (gently stir) into the custard.

13. Freeze using a domestic ice cream machine, or cover and place in the freezer, stirring every few hours to break up the ice crystals.

14. If you're using a domestic ice cream machine, transfer to a freezer-proof covered container when the ice cream has achieved a semi-solid consistency (around 15 minutes). Place it in the freezer, and continue to freeze until it is solid.

Notes:

o Lavender flowers should be available at your local health food shop.

o To pasteurise the eggs, heat the custard to 73C and maintain that temperature for at least 5 minutes. Use a cooking thermometer, though, and keep stirring! If the custard goes any higher than 76C, the eggs will scramble. Immediately cover and place in the freezer until cool.

A tip from our kitchen:

I suggest you use a simple, liquid honey. Darker or more complex honeys will have a very strong flavour, so in that case use less!

Seán's favourite Pairing:

Sauté orange or tangerine slices with a bit of butter, serve with this ice cream and garnish with lavender flowers.

ORANGE JAFFA (ORÁISTE) ICE CREAM

This is one of our earliest ice creams and has proven very popular with our customers over the years. In fact, there is a certain little girl whose first word was reportedly 'Jaffa' when demanding this flavour. It's a crowd-pleaser, with shredded bits of the Jaffa cakes so popular in Great Britain, as well as orange zest and another British invention – marmalade. Marmalade goes way back in Britain (the Oxford English Dictionary cites 1480 as the first usage of the word) and is generally made with citrus fruits -orange being the most popular option. As citrus fruits became more available in Britain in the sixteenth century, marmalade became a choice sweet. In fact, anyone who has travelled in the UK will be hard put upon to remember a traditional breakfast without the option of these preserves and toast.

Originally we wanted to make an orange ice cream, and bought a juicer for squeezing oranges. We had a bit of trouble, however, formulating an ice cream that didn't go icy from the orange juice. The marmalade came from me strolling around the supermarket, looking for something that would help boost the flavour. It worked perfectly, but needed orange zest (grated peel) to brighten the flavour. Eventually, we removed the orange juice altogether and kept it for our sorbets, to which it was much better suited. The great thing about orange zest (besides its magnificent taste) is that it uses a part of the fruit one would normally just throw away or compost, and that always is a pleasure. Anyway, we tossed some Jaffa cakes into the orange ice cream base and finally had a flavour we adored.

You may not know:

The English word, 'marmelade', comes via French from the Portuguese word 'marmelada,' which itself contains a 'marmelo' – a quince.

Ingredients:

- 130g sugar
- 5 egg yolks
- 240ml cream
- 200ml milk
- Zest (grated peel) of half an orange
- 50g marmalade
- 4 Jaffa cakes

WHAT TO DO:

1. Add the orange zest to the milk and bring to a simmer.

2. Remove from the heat.

3. Beat the sugar and egg yolks together until thick and pale yellow.

4. Slowly beat the milk into the eggs and sugar.

5. Pour the mixture back into the pan, and place over low heat.

6. Stir continuously until the custard thickens slightly (around 65–70C) and just coats the back of a spoon. Don't over-heat, though, because at around 76C you will scramble the eggs!

7. Immediately remove from the heat.

8. Sieve if you want to remove the orange zest.

9. Stir in the marmalade.

10. Transfer the custard into a small container, cover, and refrigerate until cool (5C).

11. Whip the cream until it has doubled in volume (you should have soft peaks – don't over-whip).

12. Fold the cream (gently stir) into the custard.

13. Shred the jaffa cakes into small pieces.

14. Freeze using a domestic ice cream machine, adding the jaffa cakes when it's semi-solid.

15. You can also just cover and place in the freezer, stirring every few hours, and again, add the jaffa cakes when it's semi-solid.

16. If you're using a domestic ice cream machine, transfer to a freezer-proof covered container when the ice cream has achieved a semi-solid consistency (around 15 minutes). Place it in the freezer, and continue to freeze until it is solid.

Notes:

o To pasteurise the eggs, heat the custard to 73C and maintain that temperature for at least 5 minutes. Use a cooking thermometer, though! If the custard goes any higher than 76C, the eggs will scramble. Immediately cover and place in the freezer until cool.

A tip from our kitchen:

Although you can use an ordinary kitchen grater for the zest, it is possible to buy a zester from a kitchen supply shop that gives nice, long pieces of peel that look great for decorating any dessert. When zesting, use only the outer, coloured layer, avoiding the white pith underneath. Finally, it's a very good idea to choose organic fruit when you wish to use the peel.

Seán's Favourite Pairing:

Dark chocolate and orange work very well together. This goes well with the Sachertorte.

PISTACHIO (PISTACHE) ICE CREAM

You may not know:

Pistachio is a small tree native to the mountains of Iran, Turkmenistan, and Afghanistan.

A tip from our kitchen:

Almond essence can be very volatile, and the amount given here is just a guide. You might do well to add it in tiny parts, tasting all the time!

When French people come into our shop, there are three flavours they will most likely choose – mango, vanilla, or pistachio. Of the three, the last seems to be the closest to their hearts. In the same way that you can make an Italian tourist happy when you serve a good espresso, a large percentage of French will show great delight at a well-executed pistachio ice cream. In fact, we had one French woman working in a shop next door in Dingle. Since pistachio is a flavour we rotate in and out of the scooping cabinet, she would stick her head into the shop most days and simply ask, 'Pistache?' If we had it, she'd buy a scoop. If not, we'd say, 'Non pistache!' and she would mournfully head away.

Of course in France, they generally make this flavour without any cream (and a good deal of food colouring!) What made our French neighbour so excited was the creaminess that, she told us, made it the best 'Pistache' she ever tried. Given her penchant for ice cream, we took that as quite a compliment. She isn't the only one to like pistachios – it is a nut that's hard to dislike. Seán is so addicted to them that you can usually find him by the trail of his pistachio shells. The fact that you have to shell them seems to increase their pleasure, although even without that they have the perfect flavour and crunch. In the ice cream, we have added a traditional hint of almond. The recipe calls for pureeing the nuts, and we will leave it up to you how smooth you wish to make it.

WHAT TO DO:

1. Beat the sugar and egg yolks together until thick and pale yellow.
2. Bring the milk to a low simmer.
3. Beat the milk into the eggs and sugar in a slow stream.

4. Pour the mixture back into the pan and place over low heat.

5. Stir continuously until the custard thickens slightly (around 65–70C) and just coats the back of a spoon. Don't over-heat, though, because at around 76C you will scramble the eggs!

6. Immediately remove from the heat.

7. Allow to cool.

8. Put the pistachios in a blender or food processor, adding just enough of the custard to help it mix. Blend until smooth.

9. Whip the cream until it has doubled in volume (you should have soft peaks – don't over-whip).

Ingredients

- 130g sugar
- 5 egg yolks
- 240ml cream
- 200ml milk
- 100g shelled, roasted pistachios
- ¼ teaspoon natural almond essence

Seán's favourite
Pairing:

Trois mots: Vanille,
Mangue, et Pistache.

10. Fold (gently stir) in the rest of the custard (without the nuts).

11. Add the almond essence.

12. Freeze using a domestic ice cream machine, or cover and place in the freezer, adding the pistachio puree when it is somewhat solid.

13. If you're using a domestic ice cream machine, transfer to a freezer-proof covered container when the ice cream has achieved a semi-solid consistency (around 15 minutes). Place it in the freezer, and continue to freeze until it is solid.

Yield: 8 servings

o   Make sure your pistachios are good and crunchy. If not, you can always put them in the oven at around 100C for 20 minutes or so, but keep an eye on them that they do not burn!

o   You don't have to blend the pistachios until smooth if you like the crunch. Just pulse the blender a few times to break up the nuts a bit.

o   To pasteurise the eggs, heat the custard to 73C and maintain that temperature for at least 5 minutes. Use a cooking thermometer, though, and keep stirring! If the custard goes any higher than 76C, the eggs will scramble. Immediately cover and place in the freezer until cool.

PRALINE (PRAILÍN) ICE CREAM

Christophe, our ice cream maker, came to us a month or so after we opened, looking for a job. He had arrived in Ireland from New Caledonia, a French colony in the South Pacific and has the wonderful combination of island tranquillity combined with a fierce French pride in all things culinary. In any case, although we instantly liked him, we didn't have a position going. Thankfully, he persisted. The fourth time he checked in with us, we were a bit overwhelmed in the kitchen, so we took him on one day a week to help out. As we grew busier, he was soon working full time, and he has been an anchor for the company – not only capable of hard work in the high season, but one of the guardians of the great taste of Murphys Ice Cream.

He has helped improve many ice creams, but this flavour is his. He cooked up his praline one day and mixed it into ice cream. I loved it. It is a very labour in-tensive ice cream to make, but when Christophe does get around to it, staff and customers alike gobble it up. It's one of two pralines that we make – the other being

Praline was invented in the nineteenth century by the chef of the French sugar industrialist, Praslin. He coated whole almonds with caramelised sugar and made history.

Ingredients:

- 130g sugar
- 5 egg yolks
- 240ml cream
- 200ml milk
- 100g praline pieces (see recipe under 'Candy')

smooth and perhaps slightly richer. However, this ice cream is not fully smooth, with bit of caramelised nuts left intact to give a wickedly sinful crunch. Perhaps it's an ice cream to make on an extra-special occasion. I imagine any guests you have will judge it kindly. After all, we sent it off to the Great Taste Awards in the UK, and the judges there were unanimous. It brought Murphys Ice Cream a gold medal. The credit goes to Christophe.

WHAT TO DO:

1. Beat the sugar and egg yolks together until thick and pale yellow.
2. Bring the milk to a low simmer.
3. Slowly beat the milk into the eggs and sugar.
4. Pour the mixture back into the pan and place over low heat.
5. Stir continuously until the custard thickens slightly (around 65–70C) and just coats the back of a spoon. Don't over-heat, though, because at around 76C you will scramble the eggs!
6. Immediately remove from the heat.
7. Cool completely.

8. Put half of the custard in a blender with the praline pieces and blend for about 5 seconds.

9. Whip the cream until it has doubled in volume (you should have soft peaks – don't over-whip).

10. Fold (gently stir) in the half of the custard without the praline.

11. Freeze using a domestic ice cream machine, adding the remaining custard with the praline pieces after a minute or two.

12. Alternately, add the custard with the praline pieces, cover and place in the freezer and stir every few hours to break up the ice crystals.

13. If you're using a domestic ice cream machine, transfer to a freezer-proof covered container when the ice cream has achieved a semi-solid consistency (around 15 minutes). Place it in the freezer, and continue to freeze until it is solid.

Note:

o To pasteurise the eggs, heat the custard to 73C and maintain that temperature for at least 5 minutes. Use a cooking thermometer, though, and keep stirring! If the custard goes any higher than 76C, the eggs will scramble. Immediately cover and place in the freezer until cool.

A tip from our kitchen:

The best order for proceeding with this recipe is to make the custard first, then go to the recipe for praline candy and make it while the custard is cooling.

Seán's Favourite Pairing:

If you like praline, you like sweet things, so why not top it with some caramel sauce?

STRACCIATELLA (BRICÍN) ICE CREAM

Although this is another classic Italian flavour, the customers who order Stracciatella in our shops are almost always German. 'Two balls – one Schocko (chocolate) and one Stracciatella,' they often say, for 'ball' is the literal translation of the German word for scoop (kugel). No ice cream shop in Germany would leave out Stracciatella, their favourite flavour, which is a tasty combination of vanilla ice cream with bits of chocolate. We, however, don't always have it, and that puzzles Germans greatly. It's just that there are so many ice creams we like that we rotate them in and out like a football manager with too many stars. Stracciatella is a favourite, and the Germans are not alone in loving it.

I have visited Germany often (my sister lives there), and I have eaten the Stracciatella there. I have also tried it in Italy, and a well-executed one is wonderful. It's quite a simple ice cream, but the vanilla base can highlight a good chocolate. Stracciatella is made by pouring melted chocolate into the semi-frozen ice cream while mixing, and the resulting ribbons of chocolate offer a satisfying crunch. It's an ice cream that will appeal to all ages, and it will certainly please a German if you happen to have one coming over for dinner.

You may not know:

'Stracciatella' comes from the Italian word 'stracciato' or 'torn apart.' There is also a popular Italian egg-drop soup of the same name.

Ingredients

- 130g sugar
- 5 egg yolks
- 240ml cream
- 200ml milk
- ¼ vanilla bean
- 20g chocolate

WHAT TO DO:

1. Beat the sugar and egg yolks together until thick and pale yellow.
2. Cut the vanilla bean lengthwise and put in a saucepan with the milk.
3. Bring the milk to a low simmer. Remove from the heat.
4. Remove the vanilla bean.
5. Beat the milk into the eggs and sugar in a slow stream.
6. Pour the mixture back into the pan, add the vanilla bean, and place over low heat.

7. Stir continuously until the custard thickens slightly (around 65–70C) and just coats the back of a spoon. Don't over-heat, though, because at around 76C you will scramble the eggs!

8. Immediately remove from the heat.

9. Remove the vanilla bean.

10. Transfer the custard into a small container, cover, and refrigerate until cool (5C).

11. Melt the chocolate in a microwave or double boiler.

12. Whip the cream until it has doubled in volume (you should have soft peaks – don't over-whip).

13. Fold the cream (gently stir) into the custard.

14. Freeze using a domestic ice cream machine, pouring in the chocolate in a thin stream when the ice cream is fairly solid.

15. You can also just cover and place in the freezer, and stirring in the melted chocolate once it is semi-solid.

16. If you're using a domestic ice cream machine, transfer to a freezer-proof covered container when the ice cream has achieved a semi-solid consistency (around 15 minutes). Place it in the freezer, and continue to freeze until it is solid.

Notes:

o If you don't have a vanilla bean, or if you want to experiment, you can use high-quality vanilla essence. It's hard to say how much, since different brands and types of essences vary so much. Add it to the cool custard in very small parts until you have the right amount of flavour.

o To pasteurise the eggs, heat the custard to 73C and maintain that temperature for at least 5 minutes. Use a cooking thermometer, though, and keep stirring! If the custard goes any higher than 76C, the eggs will scramble. Immediately cover and place in the freezer until cool.

Seán's Favourite Pairing:

Einmal Schocko und einmal Stracciatella in einer Waffel.

A tip from our kitchen:

When you melt the chocolate, keep the temperature as low as possible. If the chocolate is too hot, you will heat-shock the ice cream, which can lead to iciness.

TOFFEE (TAIFÍ) ICE CREAM

The first time I made toffee ice cream, I became a bit of a joke among the shop staff, who saw me stagger in a little woozy after eating such an enormous amount of both the candy and the ice cream that my body was in sugar shock. I couldn't really help myself. Toffee is such an amazing candy – glossy and rich, and I seem to be quite helpless when I make some or some is set before me. Generally now, I'm supervised when I go making toffee to make sure there is enough for the customers.

I grew up with toffees of various kinds – English toffees in white wrappers, salt water taffy, and toffee apples at farm fairs. Toffee is different from caramel in that it uses dark brown sugar or molasses along with butter. When put in ice cream, it makes for an unbelievably rich and sweet experience. I like leaving big chunks of the cooled candy in the ice cream, although I have also experimented with adding the toffee while it is still warm and letting it melt into the freezing ice cream mix. It turns the finished product toffee-coloured and gives it a uniform texture and flavour that is great if you like a smooth ice cream. This recipe uses cold toffee. Just be ready – it does stick to the teeth!

WHAT TO DO:

1. Beat the sugar and egg yolks together until thick and pale yellow.

2. Bring the milk to a low simmer.

3. Slowly, beat the milk into the eggs and sugar.

4. Pour the mixture back into the pan and place over low heat.

5. Stir continuously until the custard thickens slightly (around 65–70C) and just coats the back of a spoon. Don't over-heat, though, because at around 76C

You may not know:

It is unclear where the word 'toffee' originates, although it entered the lexicon in the nineteenth century. There are some who say it came from the Creole dialect of Louisiana.

Seán's Favourite Pairing:

Definitely Pecan Pie. Y'all come back, now.

you will scramble the eggs!

6. Immediately remove from the heat.

7. Allow to cool completely.

8. Break up the toffee candy into small pieces.

9. Whip the cream until it has doubled in volume (you should have soft peaks – don't over-whip).

10. Fold the cream (gently stir) into the custard.

11. Freeze using a domestic ice cream machine, adding the toffee when the ice cream is already quite solid.

12. Otherwise, cover and place in the freezer, again adding the toffee when it has become semi-solid.

13. If you're using a domestic ice cream machine, transfer to a freezer-proof covered container when the ice cream has achieved a semi-solid consistency (around 15 minutes). Place it in the freezer, and continue to freeze until it is solid.

Note:

o To pasteurise the eggs, heat the custard to 73C and maintain that temperature for at least 5 minutes. Use a cooking thermometer, though, and keep stirring! If the custard goes any higher than 76C, the eggs will scramble. Immediately cover and place in the freezer until cool.

Yield: 8 servings

Ingredients:

- 130g sugar
- 5 egg yolks
- 240ml cream
- 200ml milk
- 100g of toffee candy (see recipe under 'Candy')

A tip from our kitchen:

You might find it easier to break the toffee if it is cold. Put it into the refrigerator for an hour or two, then break it with a chopping knife.

WHITE CHOCOLATE (SEA-CLÁID BHÁN) ICE CREAM

We recently had a food festival in Dingle where we took out all our regular ice creams from the scooping cabinet and put in 16 shades of chocolate ice cream. It was one of the pinnacles of Seán and my chocaholic existences. We had dark chocolate, milk chocolate, spicy chocolate, chocolate sorbet, special reserve chocolate, and of course white chocolate. We have never seen so many happy people in our shop, and the two flavours that really amazed were the chocolate sorbet (recipe under 'Sorbets') and the white chocolate. The first because it offers such a massive cocoa hit, and the second because it is so silky and delicate. White chocolate makes a brilliant ice cream with a smooth consistency that is utterly sinful.

The second high point of my life as a chocaholic was visiting the Valrhona factory in France, where I went to do a chocolate course. We learned much about chocolate, including white chocolate, which can separate easily when cooking and poses special challenges. It was upon our return to Ireland that I started working on a white chocolate flavour, and we tried various versions on our very willing customers. For example you can add a little edible rosewater (not rose essence!) for a floral touch that quite a few customers rated as our best ice cream ever. You can also add a little espresso for a white chocolate mocha ice cream. These are all flourishes, however, and once you have the base flavour you might think up other add-ins. Much more important is that you use the very best white chocolate for this ice cream. Quality shows with all chocolates, but with white chocolate especially, a cheap version will likely lead to culinary disaster.

You may not know:

White chocolate uses cocoa butter, but has no cocoa solids at all.
The flavour we associate with white chocolate is actually vanilla.

WHAT TO DO:

1. Melt the chocolate in a double boiler or a microwave to about 40C.
2. Beat sugar and egg yolks together until pale yellow.
3. Bring the milk to a low simmer.
4. Remove from the heat and beat the milk into the egg and sugar mixture in a slow stream.
5. Pour the mixture back into the pan and place over low heat.
6. Stir continuously until the custard thickens slightly (around 65–70C) and just coats the back of a spoon. Don't over-heat, though, because at around 76C you will scramble the eggs!
7. Immediately remove from the heat.
8. Add the custard to the melted chocolate in small parts, mixing thoroughly until smooth and velvety. Allow to cool, then mix in the vanilla.
9. Whip the cream until it has doubled in volume (you should have soft peaks – don't over-whip).
10. Fold the cream (gently stir) into the custard.
11. Freeze using a domestic ice cream machine, or cover and place in the freezer, stirring every few hours to break up the ice crystals.
12. If you're using a domestic ice cream machine, transfer to a freezer-proof covered container when the ice cream has achieved a semi-solid consistency (around 15 minutes). Place it in the freezer, and continue to freeze until it is solid.

Yield: 8 servings

Notes:

o The boiler or container in which you melt the chocolate must be completely dry or the chocolate can clump.
o Vanilla essences vary greatly, so make sure you taste the custard and are happy with the flavour!

Ingredients:

- 130g sugar
- 5 egg yolks
- 240ml cream
- 200ml milk
- 80g white chocolate
- ¼ teaspoon pure vanilla extract

A tip from our kitchen:

The chocolate and the custard must both be warm when you mix them for a good emulsion. The chocolate will clump at first when you add the liquid, but keep adding liquid and stirring, and it will come smooth.

Recipe continues ...

Seán's Favourite
Pairing:

Serve a scoop on
a plate decorated
with rose petals.
If you can find or
make edible petals
(there are different
varieties), so
much the better.

o

To pasteurise the eggs, heat the custard to 73C
and maintain that temperature for at least 5
minutes. Use a cooking thermometer, though,
and keep stirring! If the custard goes any higher
than 76C, the eggs will scramble. Immediately
cover and place in the freezer until cool.

Sorbet Recipes

Sorbets are a great alternative to ice cream and some people wouldn't have any other frozen dessert. They are especially suited to fruits and anything where you want the underlying flavour to really shine.

Since they are made without dairy, these recipes are vegan, and they are mostly fat-free (well, except for the chocolate one!). They can be great for people with allergies to or intolerance for dairy products or eggs.

It is worth noting, however, that the sugar content generally higher than it is for ice cream.

Sorbets generally take longer to freeze than ice cream. If you're using a domestic ice cream maker, it could take up to 20 minutes for a semi-solid consistency.

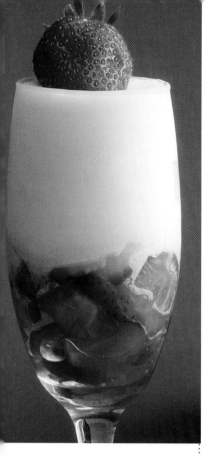

CHAMPAGNE (SEAIMPÉIN) SORBET

Of all the ice creams that we make, none seem quite as decadent as our champagne sorbet. Customers come in for it when it's time to really spoil themselves, and we're happy to give them the opportunity to do so. Of course, there are many different types of champagne, at all prices. Oddly enough, it does indeed seem to make a difference. We made this recipe with champagne costing well over 100 euro a bottle, and the sorbet was amazing. Of course it had to be, given that we had to charge 10 euro a scoop! We didn't have much trouble selling it though – one taste and people knew that it was something pretty special.

Needless to say, you don't have to spend anywhere near that amount. Choose a dry champagne that you like, and you should like the sorbet as well. Chances are if you are making this recipe, you have a truly amazing evening in mind, so you might wish to splurge a bit. The good news is that you don't have to use the full bottle for the sorbet, so you can drink some as well. Just don't get too tipsy if you're working in the kitchen!

Champagne sorbet comes out a pristine white. If you want something with a bit of colour, you can make it with pink champagne. If you do so, it is critical that you choose a dry rather than a sweet bottle, because otherwise the sorbet will be quite cloying. We have made pink champagne successfully and sold it as a limited release in selected shops, where customers snapped it up.

There is nothing we make that has the panache of champagne sorbet. It's a show-stopper. Given the high alcohol content, this is definitely not one for the kids. If you make this and have any, put them to bed, and give yourself an evening you'll never forget.

You may not know:

Although Champagne in France is known as the birthplace of sparkling wine, it seems an English doctor and scientist named Christopher Merrett invented it accidentally.

Seán's Favourite Pairing:

If strawberries are in season, use them as a garnish for the sorbet. It's a classic combination.

WHAT TO DO:

1. Boil the water and add the sugar, stirring until the sugar is completely dissolved.
2. Cool completely.
3. Stir in the champagne.
4. Add the lemon in small parts, tasting as you go. The acidity offsets the sweetness, but make sure it doesn't overpower the champagne.
5. Freeze using a domestic ice cream maker until it has a semi-solid consistency. This could take up to 20 minutes.
6. Transfer to a freezer-proof container and continue to freeze until it is solid.
7. Otherwise, simply place in a covered, freezer-proof container and place in the freezer, stirring every two hours to break up the ice crystals.
8. Since there is so much alcohol in the flavour, it might never get really hard unless your freezer is quite cold. You should also note that it will melt much faster than normal ice creams or sorbets.

Yield: 6 Servings

Note:

o   It's hard to make sorbet without an ice cream machine. You will need to interrupt the freezing process and stir. The more times you do this, the better the consistency will be.

Ingredients:

- 330g sugar
- 500ml spring water
- 250ml champagne
- 75–100ml lemon juice

A tip from our kitchen:

If you're making a special meal, you can have your glasses of champagne at the start, and simply leave enough for the sorbet. If your sugar/water mix is already cold, the timing should work perfectly to add the champagne and lemon to the mix just before your main course, put it in the domestic ice cream machine, and it will be ready for dessert!

CHOCOLATE (CÓCÓ) SORBET

If you are a severe chocaholic, the kind for whom no chocolate is dark enough and normal chocolate ice cream is too tame, read on! For this flavour packs a tremendous chocolate kick that will send the meek and timid racing for cover. To achieve this, one can not make a chocolate ice cream. It has to be a sorbet. The reason for this is that although cream supports chocolate and makes it smooth and rich, although it compliments chocolate flavour, it also dulls the cocoa edge. For a real sharp chocolate hit in a frozen treat, there is nothing like it. So placate the gentler souls with something else and make it if you are, or love, an insatiable chocolate connoisseur. It will bring bliss.

Of course, it has the added benefit in that it is dairy-free and much lower in fat than chocolate ice cream. We use a combination of dark chocolate and cocoa for this flavour. If you use cocoa only, you might get even more kick, but it will taste a bit thin. Chocolate without the cocoa will never deliver enough punch. For both the cocoa and the chocolate, you will need quality. There is absolutely no point in making it if you can't find pure, unsweetened cocoa and a good dark chocolate. Ensure the cocoa is fresh and unopened, as it goes stale quickly. We like to make it with fully organic ingredients, and you can do likewise if you wish. You should find everything you need at your local whole food shop, and if they ask you what you could possible want with so much chocolate, perhaps you could just smile. That's what we do!

You may not know:

Cocoa percentage is not always a reliable guide to how bitter or full-flavoured a chocolate bar will taste. Like grape varieties in wine, the origin and nature of the cocoa bean is a crucial factor.

Ingredients:

- 300g sugar
- 500ml boiling water
- 80g pure, unsweetened cocoa
- 300g dark chocolate (70% or darker)

WHAT TO DO:

1. Melt the chocolate in a double boiler.
2. Sift cocoa and sugar together in a heat-proof bowl.
3. Stir in the boiling water in small parts until the sugar and cocoa are completely dissolved.
4. Add the warm water/cocoa/sugar mix to the melted

chocolate in small parts, stirring until you have a smooth emulsion. The chocolate will clump at first, but just keep adding the liquid and stirring until it is smooth and glossy.

5. Cool the mix completely.

6. Freeze using a domestic ice cream maker until it has a semi-solid consistency. This could take up to 20 minutes.

7. Transfer to a freezer-proof container and freeze until it is solid.

8. Otherwise, simply place in a covered, freezer-proof container and place in the freezer, stirring every two hours to break up the ice crystals.

9. Remove from freezer and allow to thaw for about 15 minutes before serving.

10. Enjoy!

A tip from our kitchen:

If you wish to vary this recipe, the easiest way is to buy flavoured chocolate bars (orange is one of our favourites), of which there is usually quite a variety. Just make sure the chocolate is dark!

Seán's Favourite Pairing:

Chocolate sorbet is absolutely stunning with candied orange peels or sprinkled with grated coconut.

LEMON LIME (TEILE) SORBET

There are people who like sweet, and there are people who like tart. Our lemon lime sorbet is both, but it will definitely appeal to the latter. In the summer, when the days are hot, there is nothing quite like the tang of citrus. Lemonade and limeade would be drinks of choice in the Deep South of America in the sweltering heat and humidity of summer. We don't have sweltering heat here often, but there is no shortage of humidity! On a July or August day, after time spent happily outside in the sun, this sorbet will refresh and delight. Maybe you will use it to top off a barbecue, as a palate-cleaning sorbet course for an elaborate meal, or just as an afternoon snack. It is as versatile as it is delicious.

We've often been surprised in the shop at who responds well to lemon lime sorbet. A child might widen their eyes in revelation, finding a taste so intense and unique that they will have no other. People who might

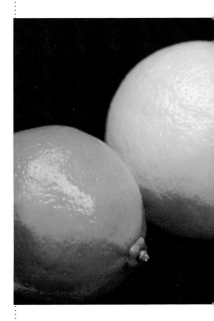

Book of Sweet Things

The best pairing for lemon lime sorbet is a hot, sunny day. Nothing more needed. Enjoy both!

Ingredients:

- 310g sugar
- 500ml boiling water
- 4 lemons
- Zest (grated peel) of 1 lemon
- 3 limes
- Zest of 1 lime

You may not know:

In the nineteenth century, British sailors were issued a ration of citrus, including limes, to counteract scurvy. Because of this, they were called 'Limey,' a nickname that spread to all Britons.

be otherwise conservative in their choices might find it irresistible. We like to use the zest (rind) of the fruit as well as the juice to give an exceedingly bright flavour, and perhaps that is what helps make it sublime. We like to leave the zest in for colour and for something into which you can sink your teeth. However, if you like your sorbet smooth, you can strain out all the pieces. Choose your lemons and limes carefully. Make sure they are ripe, juicy and organic, if at all possible, since you will be using the zest.

WHAT TO DO:

1. Zest the lemon and lime. Set aside.
2. Juice the lemons and limes – if you do it by hand, you can place a sieve over the container to catch the pips. Cover and place the container with the juice in the refrigerator.
3. Add the boiling water to the sugar in a heat-proof bowl.
4. Add the lemon and lime zest and stir until the sugar is dissolved.
5. Cover and refrigerate until it is completely cooled.
6. Add the lemon and lime juice.
7. You can leave the zest in, since it is edible and adds colour to the ice cream. If you want the sorbet without it, pass the mix through a sieve to collect and discard all the pieces of peel.
8. Freeze using a domestic ice cream maker until it has a semi-solid consistency. This could take up to 20 minutes.
9. Transfer to a freezer-proof container and freeze until it is solid.
10. Otherwise, simply place in a covered, freezer-proof container and place in the freezer, stirring every two hours to break up the ice crystals.
11. Remove from freezer and allow to thaw for about 15 minutes before serving. Enjoy!

Notes:

o   It's hard to make sorbet without an ice cream machine. You will need to interrupt the freezing process and stir. The more times you do this, the better the consistency will be.

MANGO (MANGÓ) SORBET

Mangos are considered in some cultures to be a food of the gods, and in my opinion one of the sexiest fruits in the world. Smooth, juicy, and utterly delicious, eating a ripe mango is an experience to relish. It might be messy, but it's also sensual and delivers an explosion of taste. In sorbet, mangos are just as appealing. The texture of the fruit makes this frozen treat almost as creamy as an ice cream. We have made mango ice cream as well (including an award winning mango lassi flavour), but our favourite by far is this recipe, and we're not the only ones to like it. It's proven so popular in our shops that we have added it to the list of ice cream we supply to shops in our 500ml tubs.

Mango sorbet can be served at any time or any occasion. Well able to stand on its own, it pairs perfectly with almost any ice cream or pastry. Viable as a sorbet course, it also excels as a dessert. It is light enough to be perfect after a heavy meal and flavourful enough to satisfy if the meal is simple. I am sure this versatility is why it's so popular with the restaurants we supply, and you can hardly go wrong including it in your own dinner menu. I might suggest that because the fruit originated in Asia, it's especially great with Indian or Thai food. If you've cooked up a spicy curry, then mango sorbet served after will cool, balance and restore the taste buds as well as sweeten the evening.

You may not know:

The mango is a symbol of love in India and thought to be an aphrodisiac in Southeast Asia.

WHAT TO DO:

1. Add the boiling water to the sugar in a heat-proof bowl.
2. Cover and refrigerate until it is completely cool.
3. Peel and slice the mango.
4. Juice the orange and lemon.
5. Combine the lemon and orange juice with the mango in a blender or food processor and blend thoroughly.
6. Add to the cooled sugar syrup.
7. Freeze using a domestic ice cream maker until it has a semi-solid consistency. This could take up to 20 minutes.
8. Transfer to a freezer-proof container and freeze until it is solid.
9. Otherwise, simply place in a covered, freezer-proof container and place in the freezer, stirring every two hours to break up the ice crystals.
10. Remove from freezer and allow to thaw for about 15 minutes before serving. Enjoy!

Yield: 8 Servings

Note:

o   It's hard to make sorbet without an ice cream machine. You will need to interrupt the freezing process and stir. The more times you do this, the better the consistency will be.

Ingredients:

- 300g sugar
- 500ml boiling water
- 2 ripe mangos (approx. 300g each before they are peeled and pitted)
- Juice of 1 orange
- Juice of 1 lemon

A tip from our kitchen:

The best mangos by far I have bought in Ireland were from an Asian/African food store. You might check out your local one! The mangos you use must be soft and ripe!

Seán's Favourite Pairing:

According to my son Conor, if you're making a baked cheese cake, think mango sorbet!

Ingredients:

- 350g sugar
- 600ml spring water
- 350ml red wine (I like to use a Merlot)
- 225ml fresh orange juice
- Juice of half a lemon
- 2 cloves
- 1 tablespoon cinnamon
- ½ teaspoon nutmeg

MULLED WINE (FÍON) SORBET

The idea for this flavour came from Ard Bia Café in Galway, who asked for a mulled wine sorbet for their Christmas menu. It sounded like a brilliant idea, so we set about making it, which wasn't too much of a trial. I love hot alcoholic drinks, including mulled wine, in the winter. Simply smelling the spices in the cooking wine is enough to put me in the Christmas spirit and bring up all sorts of memories of the holiday season. It's not only Christmas. My parents always have a party in the early evening of New Year's eve to watch the fireworks over the bay in Dingle from the comfort of their porch, and my job has always been to make mulled wine for the occasion.

I couldn't see any reason that a sorbet wouldn't be just as tasty, and so it proved. We often serve it in our shops in the build-up to Christmas. With the cold weather, it's nice to have the warmth of the spices and wine in an ice cream. Since it's a sorbet, it's light enough to serve after a heavy Christmas meal.

WHAT TO DO:

1. Combine the sugar, water, wine and spices and cook over low heat, stirring occasionally for about 1/2 hour, maintaining at a low simmer.

2. It should reduce to 1 litre of volume.

3. Strain to remove the cloves.

4. Cool completely.

5. Stir in the orange juice and lemon.

6. Freeze using a domestic ice cream maker until it has a semi-solid consistency. This could take up to 20 minutes.

7. Transfer to a freezer-proof container and freeze until it is solid.

8. Otherwise, simply place in a covered, freezer-proof

container and place in the freezer, stirring every two hours to break up the ice crystals.

9. Remove from freezer and allow to thaw for about 15 minutes before serving.

10. Serve garnished with a slice of orange.

Yield: 8 Servings

Notes:

o It's hard to make sorbet without an ice cream machine. You will need to interrupt the freezing process and stir, or you will be left with a block of ice! The more times you do this, the better the consistency will be.

o I think it looks well served in small wine glasses.

A tip from our kitchen:

If you have already made mulled wine for a Christmas party and have enough left over, don't throw it away! You can simply add the 350g sugar (subtracting a corresponding percentage to however much you have already used) to 950ml of your warm mulled wine and stir until the sugar is dissolved. Cool it, freeze it, and voilà! It's the best sort of recycling!

Seán's Favourite Pairing:

Try it with a poached pear!

RASPBERRY (SÚ CRAOBH) SORBET

What can I say about our raspberry sorbet? It has become such a classic, and its popularity has increased to a point we never could have imagined. Back in the early days when we started, sorbets hardly existed in Ireland outside of upscale restaurants, but Seán and I adored them. Since we both have a passion for raspberries, it was a natural flavour to make. We did so, and it has never since left our scooping cabinet. We knew it was a winner because of the stories that filtered back. Adults fell in love with it, and that word would be too weak to describe the reaction of some children. Customers who lived in Dublin would appear in the off-season and tell us that their son or daughter had badgered them so badly about the raspberry sorbet that they had cleared their schedule and driven all the way to Dingle to appease them. This was not a one-off occurrence. It happened multiple times with different families.

Raspberry is a regal fruit – both the colour and taste are so deep and intense that I consider it the king of all berries. It's perfect for a sorbet, where the experience of the fruit is unencumbered by distractions. The ingredients are simple – water, sugar, raspberries, and a bit of lemon or lime. Outside of eating fresh raspberries off the vine, it will be hard to find a raspberry experience so potent. When we launched our tubs, raspberry sorbet was naturally among our first flavours. It sold slowly to begin with, but as people tasted it, the volume grew dramatically. It's now one of our top sellers, and I'm sure the tubs placed around the country have saved families many unplanned trips back to Dingle or Killarney. This sorbet is precious to me. Enjoy!

You may not know:

Raspberry seeds have been found in archeological digs of Roman sites in England, showing that the Romans valued them so much that they brought the plants along as they built their empire!

WHAT TO DO:

1. Put the sugar in a sauce pan.
2. Pour the boiling water over the sugar and stir until the sugar has dissolved.
3. Add the raspberries and bring to a boil. Turn off the heat.
4. Stir it to break up the raspberries, then cover and place in the refrigerator until cool.
5. When it's fully cool, add the juice of the lemons or limes.
6. Freeze using a domestic ice cream maker until it has a semi-solid consistency. This could take up to 20 minutes.
7. Transfer to a freezer-proof container and freeze until it is solid.
8. Otherwise, simply place in a covered, freezer-proof container and place in the freezer, stirring every two hours to break up the ice crystals.
9. Remove from freezer and allow to thaw for about 15 minutes before serving.

Yield: 6 Servings

Note:

o It's hard to make sorbet without an ice cream machine. You will need to interrupt the freezing process and stir, or you will be left with a block of red ice! The more times you do this, the better the consistency will be.

Ingredients:

- 250g sugar
- 350ml water
- 325g fresh, ripe raspberries
- The juice of 2 lemons or 4 limes

A tip from our kitchen:

We use lemon for the sorbet in our shops and for our tubs, but lime can also be wonderful. If you like it as much as I do, you'll be making this recipe more than once, so maybe you can try both! If you don't have a juicer and squeeze them by hand, place a sieve over the bowl or other container to catch the pips.

Seán's Favourite Pairing:

Pair this with vanilla and make raspberry ripple.

TANGERINE AND LIME (TAINSÉRÍN) SORBET

I was in Mallorca earlier this year, and the orange groves were a delight to visit. In fact I can recommend the entire island! Not only is there beautiful scenery, but I had some utterly delightful meals. A specialty is their orange ice creams and sorbets, and they shouldn't be missed. Here at Murphys, we've made orange ice creams and sorbets, including of course our Orange Jaffa. I think my favourite, however, is this one – a lovely variation on the classic theme. I like to use tangerines instead of oranges because they tend to be more tart and impart a slightly richer flavour to the sorbet. The lime adds tang and makes this another great summer dessert.

There is quite a bit of juicing to be done here, so it will help if you have a electric juicer at home. If not, you can buy a simple hand one or just get squeezing (you can use a sieve over the container to catch the pips). The scent of the fruit will soon fill your kitchen, an aroma not so dissimilar from the orange groves. When you're done, you will have a bright yellow sorbet to cool you down from your efforts. The lime adds an unbelievably fresh taste that makes this a very refreshing sorbet.

You may not know:

The tangerine takes its name from 'Tangiers' in Morocco, the port from which they were first shipped to Europe.

Seán's Favourite Pairing:

This, of all of our sorbets, is my favourite for a palate-cleansing sorbet course. So pair it with a decadent meal!

Ingredients:

- 280g sugar
- 375ml boiling water
- 500ml tangerine juice (approx. 10 tangerines)
- 150ml lime juice (approx. 3 limes)

WHAT TO DO:

1. Pour the boiling water into the sugar and stir until the sugar is completely dissolved.
2. Cool completely.
3. Juice the tangerines and limes.
4. Stir the tangerine and lime juice into the cooled sugar syrup.
5. Freeze using a domestic ice cream maker until it has a semi-solid consistency. This could take up to 20 minutes.
6. Transfer to a freezer-proof container and freeze until it is solid.

7. Otherwise, simply place in a covered, freezer-proof container and place in the freezer, stirring every two hours to break up the ice crystals.

8. Remove from freezer and allow to thaw for about 15 minutes before serving.

Yield: 6 servings

A tip from our kitchen:

If you peel the tangerine carefully, you could use the peels as I have done (see photograph) for serving it!

Sauces

Seán and I love to dress up our ice cream. These sauces are a great starting point, and they can be used to enhance many desserts.

Feel free to add your own twist – once you have made chocolate sauce, there is no reason you couldn't add a taste of whisky or port. Likewise the raspberry coulis could be blackberry, strawberry, or many other fruits …

ALCOHOLIC TOPPINGS

Alcohol and ice cream make very adult and heady desserts. You can either pour the drink into a glass and then add ice cream or else serve a shot over ice cream as you would a sauce.

My top ten combinations are:

1. Chocolate ice cream with orange liqueur
2. Coffee ice cream with Irish cream liqueur
3. Vanilla ice cream with coffee liqueur
4. Mango sorbet with tequila and a bit of lime
5. Raspberry sorbet in a glass of champagne
6. Cognac with almost anything
7. Black currant sorbet with Irish stout
8. Chocolate with whiskey
9. Lemon lime sorbet with vodka
10. Port with just about anything.

I'm sure you can think of many more!

CARAMEL SAUCE

We use a lot of caramel sauce in our shops. It goes on sundaes, over ice cream and in lattes. It's a silky, sweet concoction that can make most ice creams even more special. Making it is not so easy, it takes practise, but it's worth it when you see the smiles on people's faces!

Working with sugar for me is one of the most amazing experiences – almost magical. You have this white, hard substance that dissolves into a clear liquid, sweetens everything it touches, turns into candy when cooked to a certain temperature, turns golden when cooked even higher, and it can be spun, pulled and hardened. In all its various forms, it provides happiness to people every day (hopefully in moderation!).

Sugar syrup was used by the Phoenicians and Egyptians for medicinal purposes, and for centuries it remained so valuable and expensive that it was a luxury reserved for the rich and powerful. The Crusaders brought the first sugar back to Europe along with numerous enlightening discoveries learned from the Arabs. I am surprised and grateful that they didn't eat it all on the long trip back home. Otherwise, we might still be working with honey, and although I love honey, it doesn't make such a good caramel sauce!

Please take care when making this recipe, especially if there are kids around, because melted sugar is dangerously hot! Use a pan with high sides to avoid splatter.

You may not know:

Sugar cane is actually a giant grass, and is native to the Ganges Delta in India, from where it spread to the Middle East.

WHAT TO DO:

1. Combine the milk and the cream in a single jug or measuring cup.
2. Pour the water in a medium-sized, high-sided, thick-bottomed saucepan and distribute the sugar evenly over the water.
3. Place over medium/high heat without stirring, until the sugar has dissolved.

Ingredients:

- 200g sugar
- 45ml (3 tablespoons) water
- 150ml milk
- 50ml cream

Recipe continues …

Book of Sweet Things

A tip from our kitchen:

If you don't want to use refined sugar, it is possible to caramelise almost any sugar, including fructose. It tends to curdle milk, however, so the best way to make fructose caramel is to leave away the cream and substitute apple juice for the milk.

4. If the sugar forms a crust on top, don't start stirring! Place a lid over the saucepan for a few minutes until the sugar is dissolved.

5. Continue cooking until it turns a deep amber colour, stirring it gently if it browns only at the edges.

6. Take off the heat, wait a few seconds, then add the milk and cream in a single quick pour, stirring vigorously with a whisk.

7. Be prepared – the sugar will clump up, but continue stirring until the sauce is smooth.

8. If you have trouble dissolving all of the sugar bits, return it to the heat and keep stirring until it is smooth.

9. Pour the caramel into a heat-safe container.

10. Serve warm or cold.

Notes:

o   You can freeze caramel sauce and thaw it for later use.

o   Sugar dissolves in water, so add water to the pan and heat it. Pour it out before you start cleaning.

o   It should last for three days in the refrigerator (if you are good at practising restraint).

CHOCOLATE SAUCE

We spend a lot of time at Murphys Ice Cream talking about chocolate, and our chocolate sauce has been the subject of management meetings. Of course, these meetings have been some of the most enjoyable ever, since invariably they involved bringing out different variations of our chocolate sauce, ice cream, and a pile of spoons with which to eat it. Then the discussion starts – does it have enough cocoa hit? Is this brand or variety of chocolate better in the sauce than the other? Will it satisfy both seasoned chocaholics and young children? Does it need more cream? More or less sugar? Is it thick enough? Does it hold its form on the ice cream? We taste and taste until we are too stuffed and chocolate-addled to continue. Most of the time we agree unanimously, which is a bit surprising, given the different preferences of people when it comes to chocolate.

My point with this is that we take our chocolate seriously, and our chocolate sauce is a crucial part of many of our desserts, including sundaes and banana splits. There are many ways you can make it, and this recipe is designed specifically to go with ice cream, which is why we never taste it on its own. Chocolate sauce for ice cream needs more punch and less sweetness. It has to stand up to even the strongest flavours

You may not know:

There is a New York Cocoa Exchange. Cocoa futures are also traded in London.

A tip from our kitchen:

To save time on melting the chocolate, you can boil water in an electric kettle, then add it to the double boiler.

Ingredients:

- 150g dark chocolate (70%)
- 75ml cream
- 20g pure, unsweetened cocoa (we use organic)
- 175ml milk
- 75g sugar

and come out brightly. I think this version does all of that, and we've been serving it to happy customers for about a year now. Mind you, I'm sure we'll have another chocolate sauce management meeting again soon. The sauce might not really need improvement, but the meetings sure are fun!

WHAT TO DO:

Follow these instructions carefully if you want a velvety, glossy result:

1. Melt the chocolate in a double boiler to between 34 and 45C (you can use a mixer bowl in larger pot with simmering water in it).
2. Mix together the sugar and cocoa.
3. Put in a pan with the milk and warm to about 45C until the sugar is dissolved.
4. Add the milk mixture to the melted chocolate in small parts, mixing in between, until it's incorporated. Keep adding the warm milk and then stirring until you have a smooth, glossy emulsion. (The chocolate will clump at first and look dreadful, but don't worry, trust the process!)
5. Stir in the cream.

Yield: 425ml sauce

Notes:

o   If you want the chocolate sauce to taste good, use good quality chocolate!
o   The sauce will keep for three days if refrigerated.
o   You can freeze the sauce if you want and thaw it for later use.

HOT FUDGE SAUCE

Hot fudge sauce is a very American addition to a dessert, and it is something that I miss from time to time. I like chocolate sauce, but hot fudge is thicker and more decadent. Butter is the primary difference, although we also use more cocoa. As children, we spooned it over our ice cream, and it kept its shape as the ice cream melted – a thick, luscious addition. If we finished the ice cream, Seán would polish off any unfinished fudge.

Hot fudge recipes can be very time-consuming to make. Traditionally you put the sugar and chocolate in a double boiler and cook them for a long time until the sugar has dissolved. I don't usually believe in short cuts when it comes to recipes, but I think I've found a way to make it faster with no loss in quality.

Hot fudge is great if you're feeling a bit down and need that extra bit of pampering. It's so self-indulgent it's almost primal!

WHAT TO DO:

1. Melt the butter and chocolate in a double boiler over simmering (not boiling) water.

2. Add the cocoa and stir until it is completely integrated.

3. Keep the chocolate mix warm in the double boiler.

4. Combine the sugar, milk and cream in a saucepan over medium heat, stirring until the mixture boils. Remove from the heat.

5. Add the hot milk mixture to the warm chocolate mixture as follows – add one sixth of the liquid, stir until the liquid is completely incorporated, then add the next sixth, stirring again, and continue thus until all the liquid has been added.

6. It will clump at first, and it may separate, but keep adding a bit of the milk mixture and stirring it in until the sauce is glossy and smooth.

Ingredients:

- 150g 70% chocolate
- 100g butter
- 100g cocoa
- 300g sugar
- 150ml cream
- 100ml milk

Recipe continues …

Book of Sweet Things

You may not know:

Chocolate was so valuable to the Aztecs, that when they conquered other tribes, they demanded tributes paid in cocoa beans.

A tip from our kitchen:

Ensure that the water in your double boiler does not touch the upper container that contains the chocolate. Otherwise the chocolate can burn.

7. Serve the fudge sauce warm over ice cream!

Notes:

o   This makes quite a bit of sauce, but you can keep it refrigerated for a couple of weeks (if you have that kind of self-control!).

o   You can also freeze it and thaw it for use at a later date.

RASPBERRY COULIS

Fruit coulis (sauce) perks up a dessert. Not only is it colourful, but it also tastes great. Most high-end restaurants will serve desserts with coulis for its decorative qualities and flavour. In our own shops, we serve coulis with cake and in fruit sundaes. There are many different colourful fruits that make a great coulis – mango, strawberry, blackberry, passion fruit, blueberry, and of course raspberry – to name just a few. We have always been partial to berries – we had six different varieties in our garden growing up, and we would eat them until our tummies hurt. Of course, berries also go well with ice cream, and that is where a coulis comes in. To make it, you generally use 10% sugar to fruit with a bit of lemon or lime juice to preserve it and to add a little tang.

My favourite of all is raspberry. Its brilliant red colour can make the simplest dessert look great, and the taste is seduction itself. If you have your own raspberries or come across a punnet of raspberries and are wondering how they might fit into your dessert plans – wonder no further! Use the recipe below and then decorate to your hearts content. You can drizzle it over ice cream, create artistic effects on a plate of chocolate tart, whip it into some cream, or soak it into a sponge for a raspberry-tinted layer of a cake. Any way you use it, it's bound to be a great addition. The best part is that it couldn't be simpler to make!

You may not know:

Raspberry juice was used in Medieval Europe for paintings and to illustrate manuscripts.

WHAT TO DO:

1. Combine all the ingredients in a blender or food processor and puree until smooth.
2. Pass through a fine sieve using a rubber spatula or the back of a wooden spoon until only the seeds are left.
3. Discard the seeds.
4. Enjoy!
5. Yield: 150 ml coulis

Ingredients:

- Small punnet (125g) fresh raspberries
- 2 tablespoons sugar
- 1 teaspoon fresh lime juice

Recipe continues ...

A tip from our kitchen:

If you really want to make this and can't find fresh raspberries, you can use frozen raspberries, but allow them to thaw before you start.

Note:

o   It will last around 3 days if refrigerated, but I suggest you eat it straight away!

Ice Cream Desserts

Ice cream, for Seán and myself, is very much a special treat. If you want to make it even more special to celebrate a birthday, a promotion, or simply your love for those dear to you, here are our favourite ice cream concoctions.

AFFOGATO AL CAFFÈ

One of my favourite desserts in the whole world is an Affogato al Caffè, and I just wish that more people knew about it! I'm not alone in loving it – Seán rates an Affogato as the best dessert we sell. It combines two of our favourite things – coffee and ice cream. If you make an Affogato with chocolate ice cream, it includes three! It's not complex or complicated, it's just plain delicious. It can be served with cream, but that is not my preference.

When first I came across an Affogato al Caffè in Italy, I thought I was in heaven. In some ways, it is the opposite of a coffee float, which is also delectable. In making a coffee float, you would take a mug of coffee and add a scoop of ice cream. It might be a better interpretation of the Italian – the ice cream really is 'drowned' by the coffee. Made with espresso, an Affogato is more of an ice cream lover's treat, albeit with a strong kick of coffee. In terms of making it, it's dead easy. You take a scoop of ice cream and pour over a hot shot of espresso. Then, if you're like me, as you eat the melting ice cream and spoon up the cooling espresso, you give a little prayer of thanks for such an amazing invention.

You may not know:

Affogato means 'drowned.' Of course in terms of the dessert it means 'drowned in coffee.'

Ingredients:

- 1 scoop ice cream
- 1 long shot (40ml) espresso

Seán's 5 Favourite Ice Creams to Put in an Affogato:

- Vanilla
- Irish Cream Liqueur
- Chocolate Whiskey
- Cinnamon
- Praline

WHAT TO DO:

1. Scoop a scoop of ice cream.
2. Put it in a small coffee cup (that's the way we like to serve it, but you could also put it in a bowl).
3. Pour a hot shot of espresso (we use a single shot run long – an espresso lungo) over it.

Note:

o   In our shops, we serve the shot of espresso on the side and let the customer do the pouring, which you might want to do if you have guests.

BANANA SPLIT

In our shops, when customers want to celebrate a very special occasion, when they wish to treat themselves to the ultimate ice cream experience, they order a banana split. Big enough to satisfy the greatest ice cream hunger, it can also be shared for a romantic ice cream experience.

It seems the banana split was invented by a fellow named Strickler in Latrobe, Pennsylvania in 1904, although there is a bit of controversy about the fact. In any case, it is an easy and indulgent treat to prepare, and the combination of the fruit, ice cream, and warm sauce, makes it a delight to consume.

WHAT TO DO:

1. Take a banana and split it lengthwise.
2. Put it in a banana split boat if you have one or otherwise a long dessert bowl.
3. Pile on three scoops of ice cream (traditionally vanilla, chocolate and strawberry, although we substitute honeycomb in our shops.) Don't make them too big – it's already a big dessert!

Ingredients:

- 3 small scoops of ice cream
- 1 banana
- 50–100ml cream, whipped
- 3 tablespoons chocolate sauce (see recipe under 'Sauce')

You may not know:

In our shops, we call our banana split 'Titanic,' since it is big and sort of looks like a boat. However, there are only three scoops of ice cream and three cookie 'smokestacks.' Many customers have pointed out the Titanic had four! It's a great conversation starter.

Recipe continues …

Book of Sweet Things

The original banana split contained pineapple as an additional topping, which makes for an even fruitier experience. You can go even further if you substitute raspberry coulis for the chocolate sauce.

4. Pour some warm chocolate sauce over the ice cream (you could also use caramel sauce, or anything else that takes your fancy).

5. Top it with whipped cream.

6. Sprinkle chocolate shavings or sprinkles, nuts, or other toppings you enjoy over the cream.

7. A long biscuit stuck in each scoop of ice cream completes the effect.

Now it's time to bring out the spoon!

CRÊPES

You may not know:

Crêpes come from Brittany in France. The word comes from the Latin 'crispa', meaning 'crinkled'.

I love eating an ice cream wrapped in a crêpe. The textural sensation is delightful, and although relatively simple, it's a rather sophisticated dessert. We like to serve crêpes in our shops over the winter, when customers still want ice cream but crave something warm as well. This way they can have both, and they are never disappointed.

Crêpes are quite easy to make at home, and you can use the same crêpes to make a main course (a tasty filling is fresh baby spinach, cheese and toasted pine nuts). If you make them or pancakes regularly, I highly recommend getting a crêpe pan. It shouldn't be expensive, and what a difference it makes! Not only do they come out the perfect size every time, but they cook more evenly and don't stick.

WHAT TO DO:

1. Combine flour, sugar and salt.
2. Add milk, water, butter and eggs and process until smooth (use a food processor ideally or electric mixer).
3. Leave to settle in the fridge for at least an hour.
4. Warm the pan over medium heat, then spoon in the crêpe mixture, tilting the pan until you have a uniform, thin layer.
5. Cook over medium heat until the edges begin to lift away from the pan.
6. Flip and cook on the other side until done.

Yield: 10 Servings

To make an ice cream crêpe:

1. Warm a plate.
2. Slide the crêpe onto a warmed plate.
3. Scoop a scoop of ice cream into the centre of the

Ingredients:

- 150g non-rising flour, sifted
- 40g butter, melted
- 15g sugar
- 250ml milk
- 75ml water
- 3 eggs
- ¼ teaspoon salt

Seán's 5 Favourite Ice Cream Crêpes:

- Raspberry Sorbet with chocolate sauce
- Chocolate whiskey ice cream with chocolate sauce
- Chocolate ice cream with raspberry coulis
- Vanilla ice cream with chocolate sauce (a classic)
- Praline ice cream with caramel sauce

Recipe continues ...

If you want to make them all at one time, put a stack on a plate with waxed paper in between them to keep them from sticking. You can keep them warm in the oven on low heat.

crêpe and roll the crêpe around it.

4. I highly recommend topping it with chocolate sauce.

5. Serve immediately. The ice cream will cool the crêpes very quickly.

Notes:

o   You shouldn't need any oil or butter on the pan if it is a good one. The butter in the crêpes will keep them from sticking.

o   You can add whipped cream as well, but if you do make sure you put it on the crêpe and not on the plate, as it can go sour if the plate is warm.

FROZEN BANANA POPS

Not all frozen desserts need to be high in sugar, and here's a healthy treat that is guaranteed to please the kids. It's nothing more than a banana, frozen. This might sound a bit boring, but a banana popsicle is a brilliant snack on a warm day.

I speak from great experience here. My mother often kept frozen bananas in the freezer for us when we were small, and we loved them! The best part about them is that the pleased little ones won't be bouncing off the walls from a sugar high!

Ingredients:

• Bananas
• Dark chocolate (optional)

WHAT TO DO:

1. Peel a ripe banana.

2. Cut it in half.

3. Push a plastic spoon or lolly stick into the cut end of the banana.

4. Put it/them in a freezer-safe dish and leave in the freezer for a few hours.

5. That's it! You can serve them straight from the

freezer, and they will disappear quickly.

6. If you want to take it a step further, melt some bittersweet (70%+) chocolate (generally quite low in sugar if the quality is high) or good quality dark diabetic chocolate, pour it on a shallow plate and roll the frozen pops in it. Do the rolling quickly as the chocolate will harden on immediately!

JUICE POPS

Another quick and easy sugar-free iced option is frozen juice pops (lollies). This one really brings me back to my childhood. I have many memories of hot and humid summer days that involve these treats. My mother was really into natural foods and organics, and although we were never weaned off ice cream, she tried to keep us off commercial sweets by making these. We ate them quite happily indeed.

I found a form for the pops in my local hardware store, and nothing could be easier in terms of making them. What's really brilliant is that you can choose a juice that you (or your little ones) like and make the frozen equivalent. It's hard to go wrong with that!

It's definitely worth trying them with freshly-squeezed juice. There are also many delicious organic juices that you can find in health food shops. In any case, the taste will reflect the quality of the juice, and clearly if you add a juice mix that has sugar in it, it will not be sugar-free!

Ingredients:

- Fruit juice

WHAT TO DO:

1. Simply pour the juice into the popsicle form, insert the stick, and put it in the freezer.
2. Within a couple of hours, you will have a wonderfully refreshing frozen snack.

MURPHYS MILKSHAKE

The best way to cool yourself down on a hot day with ice cream is to make it into a thick, luscious milkshake. If you drink it too fast, you even have an experience of 'brain-freeze' – the cold is actually painful. Milkshakes are enduringly popular, and there's something quite romantic about them. When I was in my teens, it would be quite usual to go to the local ice cream parlour with a girlfriend and share a milkshake. They are almost always served with two straws, and we maintain that tradition at Murphys. A shy teenage couple with a single milkshake, each drinking slowly with their own straw, their faces almost touching and their eyes locked, is one of the most delightful sights we witness in our shops.

Milkshakes are not only for teens, of course, and we sell them to all ages. They are one of the ways to make ice cream a little more festive and are often chosen for a birthday or other celebration. There are also people who would never have their ice cream any other way and who have become connoisseurs of blending two flavours in a single shake to get exactly the dessert they desire.

It doesn't take much to make a milkshake, and you can use a food processor or blender. It's a bit hard to get it smooth without a special shake blender such as we have in our shops, but there is a solution. Seán's done a lot of research on this (if you want to see him suffering 'brain-freeze' you can look up the phrase on our blog), and the best way is to make sure the ice cream is not too hard when you blend it. Then all you need is two straws.

Seán's 5 Favourite Milkshake Combinations:

- Coffee ice cream with a shot of espresso
- Vanilla ice cream with extra scrapings of vanilla seeds
- A scoop of Cookies and a scoop of Mint
- A scoop of Chocolate and a scoop of Vanilla
- A scoop of Raspberry sorbet and a scoop of Strawberry

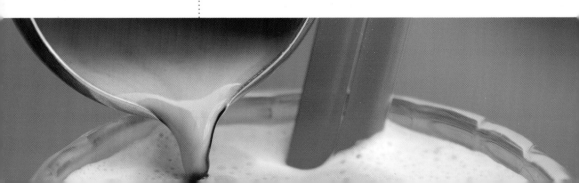

WHAT TO DO:

1. Put the ice cream and milk in the blender or food processor and allow it to soften for five minutes (blending it straight away will leave lumps of ice cream in the shake).
2. Blend until smooth on high speed.
3. Garnish with cream (optional).
4. Add two straws.
5. Enjoy!

NELL'S OLD FASHIONED FRUIT CUP

We were not the first ice cream pioneers in Dingle. Long before Murphys Ice Cream opened its doors on Strand Street, a woman named Nell Grandfield made ice cream from scratch in the very same building and delighted generations of customers. Born in 1896 to a family on John Street, Nell emigrated to England, where she worked for years as a dressmaker. When she inherited the building in the 1940s from an uncle, she returned to Kerry, happy to leave behind the needle and thread. Her uncle sold religious goods, but Nell had different ideas. She turned the shop into a sweets emporium and soon began making ice cream.

She used fresh cream from the Dingle creamery, and appreciative patrons would stop by Nell's on their way to the cinema for an ice cream or a chocolate. Twenty years after Nell shut her doors, my brother and I leased her shop, and we soon met her former customers and heard the stories. Many of them still come in to Murphys, and although our equipment is more modern, our ingredients more exotic, and we cost more than 6 pence, I do think that Nell would have approved. She was best known for ice cream served in a dish with fruit, and this is a slightly more gourmet version of her fruit cup.

Ingredients:

- 2 scoops ice cream
- 200ml milk
- Dollop of whipped cream (optional)

You may not know:

There's a variation of a milkshake called 'malted.' It's a regular milkshake with added malt powder and a real American classic.

Ingredients:

- 1 scoop vanilla ice cream
- A generous dash of raspberry coulis or cordial
- A few tablespoons of fresh fruit salad or fruit cocktail
- A wafer cut diagonally

A tip from our kitchen:

If you do add sugar to the fruit, add less than you think you would need. The fruit salad will become a lot sweeter as it sits a while.

WHAT TO DO:

1. Scoop the ice cream into a glass dish.
2. Spoon over the fruit.
3. Add the raspberry sauce.
4. Top with the wafer.
5. Devour it!

Notes:

o Try to buy local fruit that is in season whenever possible. Nothing beats it!

o Choose fruit with a variety of colours to make the salad look its best.

o Mix up the textures a bit – smooth fruits, crunchy fruits, etc.

o A tablespoon or two of cognac is a great addition to fruit salad!

o Letting the fruit salad sit for a few hours will greatly enhance the flavour, especially if you have put in some cognac. (It's a good idea to leave it in the refrigerator).

PEACH MELBA

Peach Melba is an ice cream classic, and it is sure to be a hit with dinner guests. It consists of poached peaches, vanilla ice cream, and a sauce made from raspberries and red currants, although it's usually just made with raspberry sauce.

WHAT TO DO:

1. Peel, pit, and cut up some fresh, ripe peaches.
2. Combine the sugar and water and bring to a boil.
3. Drop the fruit into the boiling water and leave for two or three minutes (I don't like to give them an over-cooked taste).
4. Strain and allow to cool.
5. Put the peaches in a dish, add a scoop of vanilla ice cream, and drizzle liberally with the raspberry sauce.
6. Garnish with fresh red currants in honour of the famous French chef and the diva!

Ingredients (per person):

- 1 fresh, ripe peach
- 3 tablespoons sugar
- 500ml water
- 2 tablespoons raspberry coulis (recipe under 'Sauce')
- One scoop vanilla ice cream
- Whipped cream
- Red currants (for garnish)

You may not know:

Invented in the 1890s by the French chef Escoffier, who was working at the Savoy in London, Peach Melba was a dish made for an Australian opera diva – Nellie Melba.

POIRE BELLE HÉLÈNE

Ingredients
(per person):

- 1 fresh,
  ripe pear
- 3 tablespoons
  sugar
- 500ml water
- 2 tablespoons
  chocolate
  sauce
- One scoop
  vanilla ice
  cream

A favourite dessert in our family, Poire Belle Hélène is simple and delicious. My parents have a pear tree growing beside their house, and this dessert always comes into mind as the fruit appears and ripens. You can, of course, use canned ones to make it dead easy, but poaching pears isn't that difficult, and they will taste better.

WHAT TO DO:

1. Peel, core, and quarter the pear (you can also poach them whole).
2. Combine the sugar and water and bring to a boil.
3. Add the pear and simmer for about five minutes.
4. Strain and allow to cool.
5. Place the pieces of pear (or the whole pear) in a dish, add the ice cream, and drizzle with warm chocolate sauce.

You may not know:

This is another dessert invented by the French chef Escoffier, who liked his musical themes. This inspiration came from the 1864 operetta, 'Belle Hélène,' by Offenbach.

SUNDAE

The ice cream sundae is an American invention, and the story I like best about its inception is that during the 1890s, when consuming ice cream sodas in chemist shops was all the rage, ice cream sodas were banned on Sundays by the preachers as being too sinful. So someone came up with the sundae as a less sinful alternative and gave it the aberrant spelling so as not to offend the men of the cloth by using the name of the Sabbath. If that was the height of sinning in the 1890s, one does have to say that those were gentler times. Of course, it's a bit confusing for me, because I can't see how a sundae would be any less sinful.

With two scoops of ice cream, whipped cream, and chocolate, fudge or caramel sauce, a sundae seems a big cup of temptation. Maybe it's down to the lack of fizzy bubbles, but I would give up ice cream sodas any day for a go at this particular dessert. I never have lost my taste for it, and usually when making one goes a bit wrong in the shops and can't be served, it will disappear between Seán, myself and our staff long before it is thrown away. It's just too much of a temptation when there are spoons around. It rates as one of our most decadent options. Interestingly enough, we do sell more sundaes on Sunday.

In the US, you would also top it with a cherry, but the cherries they used were so distasteful to me and my brother that we can't bring ourselves to include that in our method.

WHAT TO DO:

1. Take a tall glass and dribble some chocolate sauce in the bottom of it.
2. Add a scoop of ice cream.
3. Pour in more sauce.
4. Add the second scoop.

You may not know:

The birthplace of the sundae is the subject of controversy, with different US towns from Ithaca, NY to Evenstown, IL claiming ownership.

Ingredients (per person):

- 2 scoops of ice cream
- Hot fudge (or other) sauce
- Whipped cream
- Nuts, sprinkles, or other toppings
- A biscuit or wafer

Recipe continues …

Book of Sweet Things

Seán's 5 Favourite
Sundaes:

- Two scoops
  of Chocolate
  ice cream and
  chocolate sauce
- A scoop of Vanilla
  and Honeycomb
  with caramel sauce
- Mango and
  Raspberry
  sorbet with
  raspberry coulis
- A scoop of Mint
  and a scoop
  of Cookies ice
  cream with
  chocolate sauce
- Pistachio ice cream
  and Chocolate
  sorbet with
  chocolate sauce

5. More sauce!

6. Top with cream, nuts, and sprinkles.

7. Stick in the biscuit or wafer.

8. Find yourself a long spoon and dig in.

Candy and Baking Recipes

Here are a few other recipes from our kitchen, including Wiebke's stunning Sachertorte, which also happens to be gluten-free. Whether it's playing with sugar or playing with dough, these should be fun!

For any of the recipes using flour, you must use flour without rising agents, or the recipe will suffer. Most flours, including 'plain flour,' have additions. Check the ingredients – it should say simply 'Flour' or 'Flour and Gluten.'

When butter is used it should be unsalted or lightly salted, depending on your preference.

CHOCOLATE BROWNIES

You may not know:

Brownies are thought to be an American invention, and the first known recipe was published in the 1897 Sears Roebuck catalogue.

A tip from our kitchen:

Brownies can be like steak – people differ in terms of how well-cooked they like them. We tend to like ours slightly under-baked, so that they are wickedly moist and tempting.

Seán's 5 Favourite Things to Add to Brownies To Make Them Even Better:

- Toasted walnuts (stir in before baking)
- Chocolate chunks (stir in before baking)
- Coffee liqueur (stir in 100ml before baking)
- Irish cream liqueur (stir in 100ml before baking)
- Ice cream (added afterwards – not baked!)

Most people who grew up in the US love brownies. Some of my best and earliest memories involve licking the spoon clean of brownie batter in our New York kitchen while 'helping' my Aunt Carol with the baking. No matter how much batter I ate, however, there always was room for the finished brownies when they emerged steaming from the oven. I couldn't wait for them to cool!

A brownie is not quite a cake, and not quite a cookie. They can fill a pleasing niche in terms of an afternoon snack or form the basis of an elaborate dessert. They are not difficult to make and can be a fun way to spend an afternoon with the kids (and they will happily help 'clean' the spoons like we did). The dense, flavoursome result, however, is sure to please any chocaholic adult. Whenever I make them for our shops, they are snapped up in a couple of hours. Perhaps I should get around to making them more often!

If you're sceptical about brownies, you might well have come across some of the many disappointing versions. Brownies tend to be way too fluffy instead of being dense and rich, and sadly people very often use poor quality chocolate and sometimes even a butter substitute.

If you follow this recipe, you can hardly go wrong. Your only challenge will be finding chocolate that is good enough. Make the extra effort! Splurge! It will make all the difference in the world.

WHAT TO DO:

1. Preheat the oven to 180C.
2. Butter and flour a 10 inch square baking pan. Set it aside.
3. Melt the chocolate and butter in a double boiler. Mix until smooth.
4. Beat the sugar and eggs together.
5. Add the vanilla.
6. Slowly pour in the chocolate and butter, mixing all the time.
7. Sift the flour, then add, mixing thoroughly.
8. Pour the batter into the prepared pan, and bake just until cooked, 25 – 30 minutes (a knife should just about come out clean).
9. Allow the brownies to cool slightly. Then cut them into squares and transfer to a wire rack to cool completely.

Ingredients:

- 250g top quality chocolate (55% cocoa content)
- 165g butter – at room temperature
- 3/4 tablespoons natural vanilla
- 300g sugar
- 135g non-rising flour
- 3 eggs

CHOCOLATE CHIP COOKIES

It's hard to see how anyone could dislike good chocolate chip cookies made at home. Crunchy, buttery and with a little explosion of chocolate in each bite, these are highly addictive. I like them dense, so it is utterly crucial to use flour without rising agents or they will puff up and dry out! We have made these cookies from time to time for our shops, and they go extremely well with ice cream. In fact, you can even make them into ice cream using the Cookies ice cream recipe and substituting chocolate chip cookies. If you have any cookies that escape the gobbling (extremely unlikely) you could try it.

Chocolate chip cookies are great on their own or served with a glass of milk. They also make an uplifting addition to a lunch box or an afternoon snack.

You may not know:

Ruth Wakefield is generally credited with the invention of the chocolate chip cookie in 1937 at the Toll House Restaurant in Whitman, Massachusetts.

You can make your own chocolate morsels simply by chopping up a chocolate bar. As always, use good chocolate!

Ingredients:

- 135g plain flour (no rising agents)
- 115g butter
- 75g sugar
- 90g light brown sugar
- 1 egg
- ¼ teaspoon vanilla
- 150g 50% good quality chocolate chips or chunks

Seán's 3 Favourite Things to Add to Chocolate Chip Cookies:

- Toasted pecans (stir in before baking)
- White chocolate chunks (stir in before baking)
- Macadamia nuts (stir in before baking)

You can quite easily turn them into a complex dessert by perching an ice cream on top and drizzling chocolate sauce over everything. You could also create cookie sandwiches by piling a layer of freshly-made ice cream on top of a cookie, adding a second cookie and putting it into the freezer to harden. I suggest 50% chocolate for the chips, since that has the widest range of appeal, but if your tastes tell you to go darker, don't be afraid to do so!

WHAT TO DO:

1. Preheat oven to 190C.
2. Combine sugar, and brown sugar and melted butter and beat until the colour turns light.
3. Beat in the egg.
4. Slowly add flour, mixing all the time.
5. Add vanilla.
6. Stir in the chocolate morsels.
7. Spoon onto a lightly buttered baking tray.
8. Bake for 5 minutes.
9. Remove the tray from the stove (using oven mittens), and rap the tray firmly on the counter several times to flatten the cookies and stop them from rising.
10. Bake another 4 minutes.
11. Transfer to wire racks to cool.

Yield: 7 large cookies

HONEYCOMB CANDY

This is a fun recipe. Not only does making it mean that you can create Honeycomb Crunchy Caramel, our best-selling ice cream flavour, but there's a bit of wizardry involved. Transforming simple caramel into a puffy candy brings a lot of satisfaction. Once you get the hang of it, it is as actually quite easy to make, although it requires vigilance since caramel burns easily.

It is important that you take due care when making this, especially if there are children around, as sugar gets extremely hot. When you add the baking soda, it can splatter, so use a pan with high sides and don't allow yourself to get distracted.

WHAT TO DO:

1. Butter a medium-sized baking dish.
2. Sift the bread soda (using a fine sieve).
3. Combine the water, golden syrup and sugar and cook over medium heat without stirring until the sugar dissolves.
4. Turn up the heat until the mixture becomes a golden amber colour (as in the photo), stirring if it cooks unevenly.
5. Once the caramel is ready, take it off the heat.
6. Stir in the baking soda, until it is fully combined, but don't over-mix! It will froth up and more than triple in volume.
7. Immediately pour out into the baking dish.
8. Don't stir or manipulate or it will start to collapse.
9. Allow to cool fully.
10. Break into pieces and enjoy!

Ingredients:

- 400g sugar
- 100ml water
- 40ml golden syrup (about 2 tablespoons)
- 1 tablespoon baking (bread) soda

You may not know:

Honeycomb is also known as 'cinder toffee,' 'sponge candy,' and 'hokey pokey.'

Recipe continues ...

Book of Sweet Things

The sugar mixture should reach hard crack stage (150C), which you can test by using a candy thermometer or spooning a few drops into a glass of cold water, where it should immediately harden and break easily when you take it out.
 That being said, I find that once the colour is right, the temperature is right!

You may not know:

There are different method of making meringues
– pouring hot sugar syrup into the beaten egg whites is called the 'Italian' method. This recipe is for 'French' meringues.

A tip from our kitchen:

If you want to make nests, the easiest way is with a piping bag. Start in the centre, work out in a tight spiral, then build up the sides …

Notes:

o Make sure there are no lumps in the baking soda, or it might not dissolve fully!

o Sugar dissolves in water. So for easy clean-up, fill the pan with water and heat it. Pour it out before cleaning.

o Try coating the pieces in chocolate for a really tasty temptation.

MERINGUES

If, as you've been making the ice cream, you've been wondering what to do with the egg whites, here's the solution! Meringues are a lovely dessert – a crunchy puff of sweetness on the palate. They can be enjoyed on their own, with whipped cream, or with ice cream and fruit. You can shape them into little baskets or simply make little meringue drops.

Meringues are said to have been invented in the fifteenth century in the Swiss town of Meiringen by an Italian chef named Gasparini. They are made simply by beating egg whites, adding sugar and other ingredients, and then baking them. I like mine with a little hint of lemon. This recipe makes quite a bit of meringue, but since the ice creams mostly call for 5 egg yolks, it seems useful to use the 5 egg whites!

WHAT TO DO:

1. Preheat the oven to 150C.
2. Butter two large baking sheets.
3. Beat the egg whites (if using an electric mixer, do this at medium speed rather than high speed, which will take a bit longer but give the meringues more strength) until fairly stiff.
4. Beat in the sugar in a slow stream, and then add the lemon juice, mixing all the time.
5. Beat until very stiff and shiny.
6. Using two spoons, place on the baking sheet. It should make 18 large meringues, so divide accordingly, leaving a little space around the meringues to allow them to expand.
7. You can shape them as you wish!
8. Bake for 45 minutes.
9. Cool on wire racks.

Ingredients:

- 5 egg whites
- 350g caster sugar
- 2 tablespoons lemon juice

PRALINE CANDY

This is Christophe's praline recipe to go with the ice cream, but it is also a delicious candy in its own right. A story of how praline came about is that the cook of the nineteenth century sugar industrialist, Marshal du Plessis-Praslin, had an assistant who dropped a pile of almonds onto the floor. The cook, grumpy from the pressure to serve up dessert for his master, reached out to box the ears of his assistant but proved just as clumsy, spilling his pan of hot sugar. The sugar landed on the almonds. A few minutes later, a none-the-wiser M. Praslin ate them and showered praise onto his cook for such an ingenious invention. I wish all kitchen mishaps had such a happy ending!

Praline can be made with many kinds of nuts. The important thing is that they are roasted and crunchy. They are very hard to resist once made, and Christophe

You may not know:

Praslin's cook, Clément Lassagne, is said to have founded La Maison de la Praline, which still exists in the French town of Montargis.

A tip from our kitchen:

If you don't want to sauté the nuts, you can also roast them in the oven, at low temperature, until they start to brown.

always has to guard them jealously and shoo me away when I happen (by accident, of course) to wander in just after he has made them. If you make them around the holidays, you can wrap some up and give them away, for they are great little gifts – if you can bear to part with them.

Ingredients:

- 150g whole, hazelnuts (without the skin)
- 50g whole, almonds (without the skin)
- 200g sugar
- 15ml (1 tablespoon) water
- 5g butter

WHAT TO DO:

1. Sauté the nuts with the butter in a frying pan over medium heat.
2. They will start to brown after about 5 minutes.
3. Remove from the heat.
4. Spread on a baking tray.
5. Put the water in a small saucepan and sprinkle in the sugar.
6. Cook without stirring until it is brown.
7. If it starts burning at the edges, stir it!
8. Pour the caramel over the nuts.
9. Allow to cool.
10. Cut or break into pieces.
11. Store them (if you don't eat or use them all at once) in a covered, airtight container.

SACHERTORTE

We have been serving this cake since we opened our first shop in 2000, and it is a great favourite among our customers. Seán's wife, Wiebke, is responsible for all of our baking, and this is the cake in her repertoire that I love best. The recipe comes from Wiebke's Tante (Aunt) Ingrid, who lives in Kiel, Germany. She bakes this cake for every special occasion – birthdays, weddings, or simply when her friends come around for coffee. It is her passion, and this recipe has many years of her experience in it. Of course it also has years of Wiebke's care and attention as well.

The original Sachertorte comes from Vienna. Franz Sacher, a sixteen-year-old apprentice chef, was in the employ of a prince. When the head chef took ill, Franz had to cover for his sick boss and bake a cake to impress the court. He whipped up a Sachertorte and made history. Eventually he went off to work for himself, and there is still a Hotel Sacher in Vienna that bakes his original creation. At the Hotel Sacher, the cake is a little less moist than our version and would use apricot preserves (Tante Ingrid uses them as well). Wiebke, however, prefers using raspberry, and all of us at Murphys agree with her. It's a simple enough substitution if you are a purist.

WHAT TO DO:

1. Preheat oven to 180C.
2. Melt the chocolate in a double boiler.
3. Grease the bottom and sides of a 9-inch pan. Do not use flour if you want to share it with coeliacs — this is a special cake that gluten-intolerant people can enjoy.
4. Add the butter and sugar to a mixing bowl and mix for 5 minutes.
5. Break and separate the eggs.
6. Slowly add the egg yolks and continue mixing for 5 minutes.

Ingredients:

For the cake:

- 200g 70% chocolate.
- 200g butter
  – cut into pieces and slightly softened
- 15g butter for greasing baking pan
- 200g sugar
- 200g almond flour (ground almonds)
- 8 eggs
- 400g raspberry jam

For the ganache:

- 85g unsalted butter
- 225g 70% chocolate
- 150ml golden syrup
- 15ml (1 tablespoon) cognac or good rum

Recipe continues ...

7. Mix in the almond flour.

8. Add the melted chocolate.

9. At this stage don't over-mix; continue at a slow speed.

10. Beat the egg whites in a cold, dry bowl until soft peaks form. Don't over-beat.

11. Gradually fold the beaten egg whites into the dough until combined.

12. Pour the dough into the greased baking pan and bake for 45-50 minutes at 180C. Remove from the oven and immediately spread the raspberry jam over the top of the cake.

13. Leave in the baking pan for 1 hour.

14. To make the ganache, melt the chocolate in a double boiler.

15. Melt the butter over low heat in a separate pan (don't let it get too hot).

16. Vigorously stir the melted butter into the chocolate, maintaining a temperature of 35–45 C.

17. Stir in the golden syrup.

18. Stir in the cognac or rum – stirring hard until it is smooth and glossy.

19. Pour the warm ganache over the cake, allowing some of it to run down the sides.

20. Spread it gently with a spatula until it covers the entire cake.

21. Allow to cool. The ganache should set (harden) before serving.

TOFFEE

This is the toffee you will need for the toffee ice cream, but you can just as easily enjoy it as a candy. It's very dark and rich, since the recipe calls for dark brown sugar. One can, of course, make it with light brown or even regular sugar, but I like the deep flavour of the molasses contained in dark brown sugar.

WHAT TO DO:

1. Butter a small baking dish.
2. Combine all of the ingredients in a thick-bottomed saucepan.
3. Stir over medium heat until the ingredients are combined.
4. Turn up the heat and stop stirring.
5. It will start boiling.

Ingredients:

- 150g butter
- 200g dark brown sugar
- 50ml water
- 1 teaspoon golden syrup

Recipe continues …

The final product will have the consistency of the bit you drop into the cold water. If you like your toffee soft, take it off the heat when it forms a soft ball when dropped in the water. If you like your toffee hard, keep cooking and take it off the heat when it forms a hard ball in the water.

6. If it starts smoking around the edges, stir gently in a circle around the edge to keep it from burning.

7. Check if it's ready by dropping a bit of the toffee in a cup of cold water. It should be firm but not hard to the touch.

8. Immediately remove from the heat and pour into the buttered baking dish.

9. Allow to cool.

10. When it's mostly hardened, score it with a knife to make it easier to break.

Note:

o   Make sure the pan is very clean before you start. If there is residue already on the pan, it is more likely the candy will burn.

SUGAR

Coffee and Hot Chocolate

There are times when nothing will suit the mood except a steaming mug of chocolate or coffee to enjoy with the paper or with a great conversation.

Hot chocolates and coffees have been an integral part of Murphys Ice Cream since we opened our doors. Here are our favourite chocolate recipes as well as a few tips and tricks on coffee.

MURPHYS HOT MELTED CHOCOLATE

This is a classic dark hot chocolate that we serve in our shops. We sometimes call it 'bittersweet,' because we make it with melted, bittersweet chocolate. That name, however, is slightly confusing because there is nothing bitter about it. Don't expect a drink like the Mayans prepared as early as the sixth century AD – they called their drinking chocolate 'xocoatl,' meaning 'bitter water.' They drank it unsweetened, as did the Aztecs who followed them, since back then sugar only grew on the other side of the world. It was the Spanish who started adding sugar to their drinking chocolate. This made it more palatable to Europeans, and by the fifteenth century, the craze for chocolate had spread to Paris.

France's long history with chocolate is apparent by their wonderful hot chocolates, which you can still find today. I encountered my first in Paris, and for me the heavens opened and the angels sang. I couldn't believe a chocolate could be as thick and decadent, and I left the café on an absolute high. I've drunk hot chocolate around that city, and there's a little place at the back end of the Ile St Louis that serves my favourite cup. Each time I'm in Paris, I visit and leave lightheaded. Our Hot Melted Chocolate is a tribute to all of the chocolatiers and hot chocolate makers who have kept the magnificent tradition alive.

You may not know:

The Spanish explorer, Hernando Cortéz, presented the first cocoa beans to the Spanish court in 1528 and is generally credited with adding sugar to chocolate.

Ingredients:

- 125g chocolate (good quality, 70%)
- 500ml milk
- 45g sugar (2 tablespoons + 1.5 teaspoons)

WHAT TO DO:

1. Melt the chocolate in a double boiler or microwave.
2. Heat the milk and sugar together to about 45C and stir until the sugar is dissolved.
3. Add the warmed milk to the melted chocolate in small parts, mixing all the time.
4. It will clump at first, but keep adding the milk in small parts until it is smooth and glossy.

5. Warm to drinking temperature (55–60C).
6. Garnish with grated chocolate, and enjoy!

Yield: 4 servings.

Notes:

1. The quality will completely depend on the quality of chocolate that you use, so choose a good one!
2. The amount of sugar will vary depending on the chocolate. Obviously you can add more if you want it sweeter. Adding less won't necessarily make it more 'chocolate-y' as the taste buds need some sweetness to bring out the flavour of the chocolate.

EXTREME COCOA

Last winter, Seán told me it was time to revisit hot cocoa. He likes chocolate with more kick, as do some of our clientele, and it's hard to get that kick with hot, melted chocolate. Cocoa is chocolate with the cocoa butter squeezed out, and the lack of fat makes it taste extra strong. We had experimented with cocoa in the early days, for in most European countries a hot chocolate is a hot cocoa, and some of them are very good. We, however, had never perfected the recipe. Most hot cocoas (and hot chocolates) are too sweet and milky for either of us, and we set about creating one strong enough to satisfy Sean's cocoa craving.

I started playing around in production, with Seán offering suggestions and testing the results. None of the early attempts really pleased us, so I kept adding more cocoa. Seán didn't object at all, and the stronger we made it, the happier he became. We tested, and I kept adding more until we had bought out all the organic cocoa in Dingle. Eventually we were both happy, and the final result is utterly packed with cocoa. In fact, you might think it's a mistake when you're mak-

A tip from our kitchen:

You can make a version of this recipe suitable for diabetics if you use a good quality, sugar-free eating chocolate and omit the sugar from this recipe.

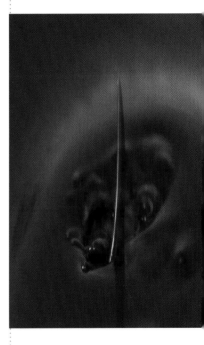

You may not know:

The Dutch invented the cocoa press in 1828. The invention brought down the price of chocolate and improved the taste of drinking chocolate by squeezing out cocoa butter.

Book of Sweet Things

You can always add more or less sugar depending on your tastes.

Ingredients:

- 125g cocoa (unsweetened)
- 800ml milk
- 225g sugar
- 1 teaspoon natural vanilla essence

ing it. It's not. This is called 'Extreme' for a reason, and it's not for the faint of heart. It will be manna for real chocaholics, and although the taste is strong, it's surprisingly light. Cocoa, after all, is very low in fat. That doesn't diminish the drink. This cocoa is thick and luscious, with a nice hint of vanilla, and it's been going down a storm in our shops.

WHAT TO DO:

1. Mix the cocoa and sugar.
2. Add the milk in small parts, stirring to create a paste, then diluting the paste until the milk and cocoa mix are combined.
3. Add the vanilla essence.
4. Pour into a saucepan and place over medium heat, stirring all the time until it reaches 60–65C.
5. Garnish with grated chocolate and/or whipped cream and enjoy!

Yield: 6 servings

Notes:

o   If you find it too strong, you can always dilute it with more milk.
o   You can freeze any excess and thaw it for later enjoyment if you have that kind of self-control.

CACAO DEL TICINO

My maternal grandmother, Edith, lived in the Swiss cantone of Ticino, in a village halfway up the mountain, overlooking the Lago Maggiore. She had moved there with my grandfather when he retired early, and they lived just a few miles from the Italian border. Their house was 500 years old with walls a metre thick, and the church in the village dated to the ninth century. The views were spectacular, the weather warm, and the mood was always relaxed. My grandfather died young, so we flew over to Switzerland whenever we could to visit my grandmother. Some of my most precious moments, especially as a teenager and young adult, were in her house and company. She visited us in New York as well, arriving with bags of Swiss chocolate, which ensured she had plenty of help unpacking. In fact, it's probably her doing that we have all ended up chocaholics.

In her own kitchen, Edith prepared simple but inspired Italian dishes. I'd help her on occasion, although more often I raided the stash of chocolate kept in her counter drawer. She liked sweet things and gave me my first tastes of zabaglione and tiramisú. When she died, we sold her house, and I haven't been back. I miss her and the house, as does our whole family. Last year, I stopped by my parent's place and found my mother looking through an ancient Swiss recipe book of my grandmother's that is long out of print. We discussed some of the recipes and found one for a hot chocolate flavoured with cinnamon, almond, and orange. It seemed a perfect drink for the winter season, so I adapted it to suit my taste for strong chocolate. It is perfect for a winter night at home by the fire, or as a great addition to a holiday meal.

This recipe is dedicated to Edith, our Nonna.

WHAT TO DO:

1. Mix the cocoa, sugar, cinnamon and orange zest.
2. Add the milk in small parts, stirring to create a paste, then diluting the paste until the milk and cocoa mix are combined. Add the almond essence.
3. Pour into a saucepan and place over medium heat, stirring all the time until it reaches 60–65C.

You may not know:

Our grandparents on our mother's side were German and fled to the US before the second world war.

Ingredients:

- 125g cocoa (unsweetened)
- 800ml milk
- 225g sugar
- ½ teaspoon cinnamon
- Zest of 1 orange
- 2 drops almond essence

Recipe continues ...

Book of Sweet Things

Beware the almond essence. It is usually very volatile. Don't use too much! It might be a wise idea to add a single drop and then taste it, adding more if you need it.

You may not know:

Myth has it that Montezuma drank 50 cups of chocolate a day. He considered it an aphrodisiac, and would down a goblet or two before visiting his concubines.

A tip from our kitchen:

Use a very fine-meshed sieve to strain it if you don't like the sensation of the remaining bits of cardamom.

4. Strain to remove the orange zest.

5. Garnish with grated chocolate and/or whipped cream and enjoy!

Yield: 6 servings

Notes:

o If you find it too strong, you can always dilute it with more milk.

o The amount of sugar will vary depending on the chocolate. Obviously you can add more if you want it sweeter.

SPICY AZTEC CHOCOLATE

I made this hot chocolate some time ago as a bit of a lark, after doing research on the origins of chocolate for an *Irish Times* article. The Aztecs, who followed on the nascent chocolate traditions laid down by the Mayans, used drinking chocolate for religious ceremonies, and it was prized at the royal court. In fact, it was considered so precious that at least one king, Montezuma, used a new, golden goblet for each cup he drank. Although they didn't sweeten it, the Aztecs spiced it up, and I thought why not try a version of the original chocolate? So I tried to formulate a hot chocolate with their ingredients, using equivalents when necessary. The most interesting component was chilli pepper, which I had seen used from time to time in serious chocolate shops.

Scarcely had it hit our shops than we sold out. I made more. We sold out again. It simply proved again that contrary to common belief, one should never underestimate the adventurousness of the Irish palate! This drink is perfect in the winter, since it is so warming. I haven't made it so spicy that the chilli burns – just spicy enough to warm you through and

through on a cold day. There's a strong dose of cardamom, which I love, and the cinnamon and nutmeg make it a perfect addition to evenings over the Christmas holidays.

WHAT TO DO:

1. Melt the chocolate in a double boiler or microwave.
2. Heat the milk, sugar, and spices together to about 45C and whisk to make sure the spices are dispersed and the sugar is dissolved.
3. Strain to remove the chilli pepper.
4. Add the warmed milk to the melted chocolate in small parts, mixing all the time, to create a smooth emulsion.
5. Warm to drinking temperature (55C).
6. Garnish with grated chocolate and/or whipped cream and enjoy!

Ingredients:

- 200g chocolate (good quality 70%)
- 800ml milk
- 60g sugar (4 tablespoons)
- ½ teaspoon ground cardamom
- ¼ teaspoon cinnamon
- ¼ teaspoon nutmeg
- Very small pinch dried jalapeño chilli pepper

Happily, there
are an increasing
amount of organic
and Fairtrade coffee
beans available
in Ireland.
Some of these are
excellent, some
are not. If you've
been disappointed,
don't give up!
Check out (and
support) small
roasters in your
area, and see what
they can provide.
We have found
Fairtrade espresso
beans and organic
coffee that we
use in our shops
and love (from
Maher's in Cork).
The more demand
we create, the
better our choices
will be. If it tastes
great and one can
feel great about it,
it's a winner for all.

A FEW WORDS ABOUT COFFEE

One of the most exciting things about our business over the last seven years has been the explosion in coffee culture. Seán and I both adore coffee and are delighted at the proliferation of coffee. When we opened in 2000, we sold 10 teas for every cappuccino or other coffee drink. For the past few years, we have been selling at least 10 cappuccinos or other coffee drinks for every tea. I don't think that we in Ireland have gone off tea. It's just that many of us drink our tea at home and coffee out. In any case, our coffee drinkers have been just as dedicated and supportive as our ice cream eaters, and they have indulged our coffee exploration and appreciated our fanaticism. We thank them!

Naturally, there are many people who enjoy coffee at home. Some, however, might find it difficult to get the result they desire. Coffee is very personal – people's taste vary wildly, but Seán and I have some definite opinions on coffee, which might be helpful.

When we make coffee in our shops, we don't do it by any magic tricks. Our philosophy on coffee is the same as for the rest of our products – use the best ingredients and use care in the process. For us, this means a lot of training for our baristas so that they can equal and often surpass ourselves.

For making good coffee at home, we suggest using a cafetière or an Italian-style stove-top espresso maker. There are loads of espresso machines sold for home use, and if you are happy with yours, great! Don't change a thing! What we have found is that it is very hard for us to get a consistently good coffee from an espresso machine, be it commercial or domestic, if you just switch it on and want a coffee. We have to make and discard up to eight espressos in the morning and let off lots of steam before our machine regulates its pressure and temperature and makes a decent one. In our experience, domestic machines are similar. Discarding espressos might make sense if you're selling a good few in a day, but at home it's wasteful.

Below, I'll explain a bit more about the cafetière and the Italian-style stove-top espresso maker, but here are a few ways we think will immediately improve your coffee:

o   Grind your beans fresh (or have them ground for you in small amounts)! It's amazing how quickly ground coffee can taste stale.
o   Get the grind right. If it's too fine and packed too tight, you will get a burned taste. If it's too coarse, the shot will be watery. A good shot of espresso should have a caramel-coloured head (crema) like a pint of porter, without being burned or bitter.
o   Use bottled or filtered water.
o   Run an espresso shot to 25ml (approx. 1oz.). Anything longer will bring in a watery taste and bitterness.
o   If you're making a latte or cappuccino, don't

Another Note on Beans:

The two most common species of beans are Arabica and Robusta. Arabica beans are considered superiour by most connoisseurs and are more expensive. Robusta beans, usually more bitter and less refined, deliver much better crema. This is one reason why better crema doesn't always mean a better espresso!

overheat the milk! There is a reason that in Italy you will never burn your mouth on a latte, and there is as reason that you're supposed to simmer milk, not boil it. When milk gets too hot, the milk proteins change and the fat separates out. It turns thin, adding to the bitterness of the drink, and it can taste scalded. We steam our milk to 57C and believe that at 60C and above, the milk has already been altered.

THE CAFETIÈRE

This style of making coffee using a French-style plunger, or cafetière, is perfect for making what most people would think of as a normal coffee. We use them in our shops, and people who like a non-fussy, drinkable, plain black coffee are delighted. There is usually far more flavour than in a Caffè Americano (from an espresso machine), and you can make it much stronger. It's a perfect vehicle for a French Café au Lait – all you have to do in addition is warm some milk and combine the milk and coffee in equal measure. It's also great for tasting an expensive or unusual bean – a Yauco Selecto, for example, or an Indian Mysore. Once you get the grind right, and figure out the right amount of coffee to add, you'll get a consistently excellent coffee every morning, noon and night!

A few tips on using a cafetière:

o   Choose your coffee carefully. There is so much variety out there. It might take quite a bit of exploration to get the bean you like. It's very unlikely that espresso beans will deliver a good coffee using this method.

o   Get the grind right. A medium-fine grind will probably work best, but it will depend on the bean and your preference. A tiny change in grind can affect the taste. If it's bitter, go coarser, and if it's watery, go finer.

o   Don't use boiling water. It will burn the coffee. You'll find you can make a much better coffee with water that is boiled and then left cool for a minute or two.

o   After you pour the water onto the ground coffee, give it a good stir.

o   Don't leave the plunger up for too long, otherwise the impurities and bitterness of the coffee will leach into the water.

You may not know:

Although many people think a Caffè Americano is a strong coffee because it comes from an espresso machine, the name means quite the opposite. Italians called it 'Americano' because it tasted like old-fashioned American coffee to them – very weak compared to their usual caffè (espresso).

People often ask us for a strong coffee, but what do they mean? The perception of strength in coffee comes from five factors, and you might consider them if you want to create strong coffee:

- The bean – some just taste stronger.
- Roast – a dark roast tastes fuller, but a light roast will be more acidic.
- Dilution – a short espresso will taste stronger, since there is less water. A cappuccino should taste stronger than a latte since there should be less milk.
- Caffeine – beans with a lot of caffeine will feel strong, regardless of taste.
- Burned or bitter coffee – this might have a strong taste but is not acceptable in our opinion.
- If you want a strong brew, you might want to play with the first four variables (and try to avoid the fifth!)

The Stove-top Espresso Maker

My grandmother in the Italian part of Switzerland never used another coffee maker, and she was certainly not alone. Virtually every house in Italy would contain one, and given that Italy is the home of espresso, that's quite an endorsement. It uses steam extraction like the big commercial espresso machine that we use, and it's a quick and easy way to get a coffee hit. The downside is that you have to keep an eye on it, since it must be removed from the heat as soon as it has extracted.

A few tips on using a stove-top espresso maker:

o Espresso beans will generally work best.

o Generally a fine grind is preferable, but again if it's bitter, use a coarser grind, and if it's watery, use a finer grind.

o Play around with how hard you pack the grind. You might find you get a better taste with a fine grind packed less or a coarse grind packed tighter.

o My grandmother always forbade the use of soap when cleaning her coffee pot. In fact, she would only ever rinse it. Most Italians say that it gets better with age.

o If you want to clean it, you could give it a little scrub every few months with bicarbonate of soda (bread soda), lemon juice, or vinegar.

MURPHY

Irelands Gourmet IceCream

Made in Dingle

Christmas
Charity Shop

PUSH

MIND
YOUR
STEP